THE Compatibility CODE

AN INTELLIGENT WOMAN'S
GUIDE TO
DATING AND MARRIAGE

Elizabeth E. George, M.A.
AND Darren M. George, Ph.D.

New York

THE Compatibility CODE

AN INTELLIGENT WOMAN'S GUIDE TO DATING AND MARRIAGE

ISBN: 978-1-60037-352-7 (Hard Cover)
ISBN: 978-1-60037-448-7 (Paperback)

Library of Congress Control Number: 2008936942

Published by:

MORGAN · JAMES
THE ENTREPRENEURIAL PUBLISHER™
www.morganjamespublishing.com

Morgan James Publishing, LLC
1225 Franklin Ave. Ste 325
Garden City, NY 11530-1693
Toll Free 800-485-4943
www.MorganJamesPublishing.com

Cover Design:
Rachel Lopez
rachel@r2cdesign.com

Book Cover Text:
Graham Van Dixhorn
Write to Your Market, Inc.

Interior Design:
Bonnie Bushman
bbushman@bresnan.net

Habitat for Humanity®
Peninsula
Building Partner

In an effort to support local communities, raise awareness and funds, Morgan James Publishing donates one percent of all book sales for the life of each book to Habitat for Humanity. Get involved today, visit **www.HelpHabitatForHumanity.org.**

PRAISE FOR
THE *Compatibility* CODE

"Myth-shattering and profoundly important! This book will completely re-write the script of how we meet and mate in North America."

—Jill Lublin, international speaker, best-selling author of
Get Noticed...Get Referrals

"The wisdom in this book is what you would hope to hear while talking with your girlfriends—only better! It contains research-based, practical solutions that help guide you to make intelligent, informed choices toward the quest of happiness with a guy that's truly right for you."

—Bonita Campbell, newlywed, Administrative Assistant,
Canadian University College

"I believe in miracles and your book is exactly the miracle I need in my life right now! My ex-husband (of twenty-seven years) and I reconnected almost three months ago. Though the physical distance between us is great, the emails, long telephone calls, and frequent visits are helping us come to understand and know each other like never before. Your book is helping me take an intellectual and logical approach to evaluating the appropriateness of recommitting ourselves to each other. I am taking my copy with me the next time we meet. The piece on knowing whether the essence of each other is a match is just one of the profound components of the book. As a matter of fact, I see no reason why people who have been married for decades would not benefit from *The Compatibility Code*! Thank you for the bottom of my heart!"

—Alice Wheaton, author of several books, including
*The Forgiveness Prescription: Get Rapid Relief from Fears,
Anger, and Resentment*

"Even though *The Compatibility Code* is a primarily a book for women who aren't yet married, I can tell you with certainty that this book saved my marriage! I married my husband when I was thirty-seven years old, and while I got lucky and found someone that I'm compatible with according to "the code," we were continually banging our heads up against one seemingly unsolvable problem. Not only did I find out what was at the root of that problem, but my husband and I are better able to handle it and many of the other little challenges to our otherwise harmonious marriage. Thank you Elizabeth and Darren for taking such care in creating *The Compatibility Code*. I hope other married couples find it as useful as we have!"

—Patricia Springsteel, Small Business Owner, Boulder, Colorado

"My wife has noted on a number of occasions that there is a terrible shortage of common sense in our present culture. Elizabeth and Darren masterfully teach us how to apply common sense rooted in solid research to the awesome task of choosing a mate. They dismantle the cultural models of mate selection and then construct a model that can successfully enable one to "pre*fix*" a relationship and avoid becoming one of the 70% failure statistics for second marriages. I have spent my career preparing people for marriage and retrofitting troubled marriages. Those who will do the work of following this model will avoid the therapeutic treadmill so common today. While the Christian counselor will want to root these concepts in a biblical frame of reference, the general public will find the social research commanding."

—Howard Eyrich, D.Min., seminary professor,
biblical counselor, author of
Three to Get Ready: A Premarital Counseling Manual

"This book takes the guesswork out of compatibility—and the emotion out of decision-making—to help you walk confidently into a lifelong, harmonious relationship."

—Kim Bérubé, Owner and Publisher,
Real Woman on the Run Magazine

"I always had the qualities that I desired in a man in the back of my mind. However, what I idealized and the type of man I was actually attracted to were quite different. Yes, I was a bad boy magnet—and didn't know how to change—until I was introduced to this book. It has completely reshaped my thinking: I experienced a paradigm shift in what I found attractive in a man. The type of man that I idealized is now the type of man that I am attracted to thanks to Elizabeth and Darren."

—Tricia Cooper, Assistant Librarian, Mary C. Moore Public Library

"What's love got to do with it? Not much, it turns out, until you read and apply the practical truths in this landmark book. Then go head first, and your heart will follow!"

—Jeff Mowatt, Best-selling author of
Becoming a Service Icon in 90 Minutes a Month

ACKNOWLEDGEMENTS

I want to first thank my husband and co-author, Darren George, for the years of research, writing, and teaching that has gone into the development and validation of this material. I admire his unbelievably brilliant mind, his vision for marriage, his invincibility, his attention to detail, and his insistence that all of our material be grounded in research, expertise, and experience.

It is with deep gratitude that I express appreciation to the following:

The legions of people and students who have contributed to the development and support of the creation of the book, from reading, editing, and suggesting titles, to giving feedback on all aspects of the material.

Briarwood Presbyterian Church, PCA, who helped equip me as a lay counselor on improving relationships.

Friends, colleagues and mentors from the Canadian Association of Professional Speakers and The National Speakers Association who inspire me and model excellence.

Dr. Patricia Ross, my fabulous editor, who helped me find my writing voice, picked me up when I faltered, and encouraged me through the labyrinth of the manuscript creation process. Her ability to hone complex material into engaging images and to convert an academic research style into a warm conversational tone was amazing.

Bonita Campbell for the hours of conversation, friendship, and reading as we re-shaped an idea, created a better image, and deleted dead words. She brought fresh perspectives and deep insight into reaching women who were going through the life-events outlined in this book.

To Phyllis George who spent many hours editing early drafts of the manuscript.

To our publisher, Morgan James and its founder David Hancock, for recognizing our vision and partnering in the process.

Special acknowledgement goes to Louise Ozment, Bonnie Rogers, Elizabeth Thomasson, Julie Vaillancourt, Kathy Ferguson, and Chris Lust. You represent a lifetime of friendships gathered from different life stages and countries. Thank you for being such a wonderful, integral part of my life. I have laughed and cried with all of you, celebrated the best and worst of times, and know that I am blessed for having each of you in my life. You are women of intelligence, grit, and fortitude, but you blend those qualities with compassion and love and empathy. I am who I am today in part because of the friendships we share; you helped give me the courage to *become*.

Perhaps I am most personally indebted to the children of the blended family that formed when Darren and I married. Marcus, Melody, and Robin read drafts of the book and brainstormed on title ideas. Their agile minds encouraged us through years of development as Marcus affirmed the usefulness of the content, Melody provided prayer support, and Robin designed our company logo. Eileen and Natalie provided hugs and kisses and endured the absence of parental attention with loving laughter and forgiveness.

I want to esteem my mother, stepfather, and late father who mentored and taught me that dreams were designed to lead you to places previously un-explored; that being a pioneer in your field was to work at the edge of what is currently known and step off into the unknown with confidence that the world was worth improving and defending; that seeking truth and knowledge are the most exquisite of all endeavors.

Finally, I want to honor the Lord for His gifting of Darren and myself to each other and to leading us to discover our shared purpose.

CONTENTS

How to Use
The Compatibility Code

Before you read anything else,
please, read this first.

PRE-CLASS NOTES

Dear Reader,

The Compatibility Code is the culmination of the past fourteen years of research and development by my husband, Darren. In the nine years since our marriage, we have taken hundreds of people through workshops on how to pre*fix* their marriage, in other words, the steps a person needs to take that will help them ask the right questions so that they can make the right decision about who to marry. We know its value and have seen the results.

While I would love for you to read the entire book, fill in the worksheets, and use some of the web references, I'm also a realist. I've been in your shoes, single, working full time, taking care of children—while trying to get up enough energy or courage to date again. Trust me, I have numerous books on my shelf too that I've referenced, even many times, but I've never actually read them cover to cover.

So, let me give you a short guide on what you should read if you absolutely don't have time to read the whole thing. Perhaps you can skim through the chapters and get the gist of most of what I'm trying to share with you. That would be great. But, I *urge* you to follow what I think of as the "short course." Consider it the quick reference guide to the code. Read the preface and the first three chapters. This outlines the first element of the code. Then read the introductions to each of the three steps of the pre*fix* process. This gives you the second element. Finally, make sure you don't miss the magic of chapter 12, the third and forever element of the compatibility code. This will give you the basics of what the book is about. If that's all you have time for, you will have a brief glimpse of what I recommend you consider and what pre-thought and actions you should engage in as you embark on your search for a significant other. (I can't lie, though. I hope that by reading the short version, you'll be so intrigued that you'll end up reading the entire book anyway.)

One more thing: in order to give you additional resources, ideas, and tools, I have developed a companion website to this book, www.TheCompatibilityCode.com, that will allow you to further explore and delve into topics of specific interest to you. There will be three types of information with an icon representing each:

 reference material, including research studies and other sources of information

 prescriptive ideas designed to help you work more deeply on personal and relationship health

tools to guide you through the process of pre*fix*ing your marriage

These icons will be scattered throughout the book, so you are welcome to take advantage of all the information that is available to you.

Happy reading!

Elizabeth

P.S. I also fervently hope that you spend the time to read through the end of "Step Two: Take a Look Outward" before you even begin to think about dating again. You'll see why when you get there...

If you absolutely do not have time to read the entire book, I recommend the short course.

SHORT COURSE

Code Element #1: Deconstruction

Code Element #2: The Prefix Process

Code Element #3: Forever Endings

ICON LEGEND

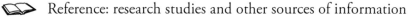 Reference: research studies and other sources of information

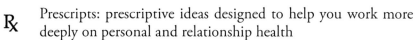 Prescripts: prescriptive ideas designed to help you work more deeply on personal and relationship health

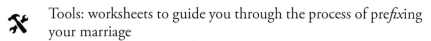 Tools: worksheets to guide you through the process of pre*fix*ing your marriage

PREFACE

I want to tell you a story very close to my heart:

Once upon a time, there was a woman in her thirties, divorced with twin daughters, who very much wanted to meet someone with whom she could share her life. Professionally she had it all together and knew a lot about personal interactions. She had completed an advanced degree in Human Resource Management and had worked as a Small Business Counselor, and in general she was pretty savvy about relationships. But in her past she had made some poor decisions with the men in her personal life, and she didn't want to make the same mistakes again so she did her homework. She received counseling, participated in divorce recovery and single parenting seminars, and eventually became a certified lay counselor in her church. By the spring of 1999, she decided that she was ready. She could go searching for her man.

Feeling excitement and yet caution she went online and joined Match. com, a very bold move for any princess at that time, particularly one from the South. This is what she posted:

> Southern Style and Professionalism. I bring to
> a friendship a tapestry in process. Threads of
> education and a profession are woven together
> by love for the Lord and my children. Images of
> travels to exotic lands mix with experience in
> international athletic competition. Bright hues
> illuminate running a Bed & Breakfast and years
> of teaching at the university level. Everyday
> portraits show an attention to detail, experiences
> from dog training to vegetable gardening, a love
> for friends, and the laughter of twin daughters.
> I would like to include the richness of masculine
> friendship as the story unfolds…someone wanting
> to celebrate the blessings of life; someone who
> enjoys the silence of companionship, who loves
> God, who savors the outdoors; who enjoys the
> arts; who loves children; who likes to engage in
> verbal sparring, who is motivated by the skills
> of his profession, who seeks the simple pleasures
> of life. A tapestry in process…

And sure enough, a missive arrived in her "inbox" from a possible, tailored-made Mr. Right. His posting read:

> Single White Male, located in Central Alberta,
> 5'10", very fit, UCLA Ph.D., articulate,
> psychology professor, pianist, Christian,
> seeking 30 - 50 year-old female. I am a strong,
> successful, competent man allowing me to be fully
> gentle and compassionate. I feel good about
> myself (with the occasional despairing moment)
> allowing me to focus my attention on you, your
> dreams, your deepest desires, and encourage you
> through your desperate dilemmas. I have a passion
> for life, for living, for growing, for giving to
> others, and so do you. I have accomplished much
> in life but am fully able to appreciate life's
> simple pleasures: a walk, a snuggle, a kiss, a
> romantic meal, a flat tire (but only when I'm with
> you!). I am deeply spiritual but not religiously
> obsessed. I care enough about myself to maintain
> a high level of fitness - a quality we can pursue
> together. Most of all I am an encourager; I love
> to work together cooperatively to accomplish

```
meaningful objectives. I enjoy physical beauty
but even more the inner beauty of heart and
spirit. I'm not average; neither are you. I'd
love to hear from you, by e-mail, phone, mail/
auto, or row boat (starting from the Arctic
Ocean, paddle down the Red Deer River …).
```

These two people eventually married and are now living a life of "happily ever after." I know this because it is the true story of how I met my husband, Darren. In our postings, we immediately noted unusually high similarities between us: academic background and profession, Christianity, psychology and business, high performance athletics, custodial parents, and musicians. In subsequent e-mails, we found that we were both able to accomplish a great deal, were logical thinkers, and that we both had a passion for excellence that had taken us to national and world rankings in athletics, achievement of graduate degrees, and the receipt of awards and publications within our professions. We also discovered that we desired for our home to be an island of warmth, love, with an atmosphere to which people would gravitate. We wanted to create an environment that embodied these ideals. As we discovered and explored those things we felt free to let romance blossom.

As we continued our online courtship, I remember Darren writing:

```
I think long-term and see, in the blending of
our lives and talents, unlimited richness and
unlimited opportunity for contribution. My desire
to touch the lives of others for good must rate
as one of my strongest passions, and with us
together I see that happening in abundance.
```

What emerged was a love that drew me across a continent. While this may sound like all hearts and flowers, we did have our own trials and challenges to overcome. We experienced the agony of intentionally setting aside the relationship and our feelings as Darren had to work through some things from his past. Specifically we chose not to have any contact with each other at all until those issues were resolved. Darren and I have since created a strong partnership that is committed to each other and to the Lord's service. My goal continues to be to script our relationship so that for us it is the romance of the century. And the beauty of it all is that in our closeness, we are energized to more fully love and contribute to our children, our family and friends. We decided early on that it is our calling and our purpose to, in some small way, create a better world around us and encourage and train others to do the same.

This book is the result of our story. In the early portion of our relationship as we discovered that we had a shared purpose we knew, even then, that we wanted to write about it together. At one point, Darren wrote, "I want to not only write the book with you but to live the book with you. I want our marriage to demonstrate that love can last a lifetime growing ever richer. Let us not only talk it, but show that it can be a reality, and with it bring hope to many." Our courtship, conversations, and dreams arose out of following the steps that I present to you here in these pages, the steps I would like to guide you through.

To help us develop the code for compatibility, we have spent the years since our courtship running seminars covering the subject matter of pre*fix*ing marriages. These seminars have blossomed into Pre*fix* Solutions Inc., the company we created to house our vision. Everything that we do now, including my speaking and this book, is with the goal to change the paradigms in North America about the way people meet, date, and select marriage partners. Culturally, our current path of developing "feelings" for an individual first and then trying to determine if they are "right" for us has led to grief and tragedy.

Our goal is to help people understand themselves better by encouraging them to "take a look inward," to help them craft a picture of an ideal mate by getting them to "take a look outward," and then finally to give them tools for "taking a look together" in their dating conversations. If we can encourage people to do that, then they will be more likely to recognize the "right" individual when he or she comes along, and, more important, be able to apply good relationship decisions before their emotions take control.

Living a marriage of purpose and passion is an exquisite joy. My goal is that by understanding and following the steps of the pre*fix* process outlined here in *The Compatibility Code*, you can find that joy as well.

MARRIAGE 101
Unscrambling the Fairy-Tale Model of Marriage

I n order to properly pre*fix* your marriage, it is vital to first uncover the main assumptions we currently hold in our culture about marriage. What ideas about marriage influence the decisions we make about potential mates? Where do these ideas come from? If our old model of choosing a mate is coming up short, creating challenged and ill-fated marriages, then, what does an ideal marriage look like? The first element of the compatibility code deconstructs what's wrong with our current ideas about marriage and then reconstructs what goes into making an excellent marriage. It gives you background information, and the things you need to know before you start. In school, we call them prerequisites, the basic classes you need to take before you get into the higher levels of your selected area of study. Here, they are simply the basics, something to get you thinking about why you've done things the way you have for so long. Once you have considered the basics, I will start giving you the tools to make more intelligent decisions and to point you in the right direction toward a successful marriage, one that truly brings you lasting happiness.

• Chapter 1 •

THE FAIRY-TALE MODEL
The Myth of "Prince Charming"

We all know the basic story. There is a young beautiful girl, often a princess in disguise, who longs for her prince charming to come and rescue her. She's bravely facing a situation in which she's helpless—a nasty stepmother, an evil charm that keeps her asleep. Often she's trapped in a castle protected by a dragon and can't get out (gasp!). These are the fairy tales that we grew up with and listened to as we drifted off to sleep, stories that we loved because the princess was beautiful no matter what rags she was wearing. More important, the princess was always rescued and lived "happily ever after" with the most handsome man in the kingdom, and it was implied that this "prince" would take care of all her physical and emotional needs. The last page in the storybook was a golden picture of the absolutely perfect couple, hand in hand, floating down the steps of the chapel, newly married, with a look of bliss that you knew would last a lifetime.

As children we believed the stories were about real people and that they really happened; we didn't question the fairy tale. By our teenage years, while we knew those well-thumbed storybooks were merely tales, we continued to hold up the story line, mentally at least, as the pattern to be followed. In our heart of hearts, we wished it could be true and we longed to be swept off our feet by our own perfect prince and be carried off on his magnificent white stallion into the sunset, with our hair flowing in the wind. Later still as we moved into the life stage where we considered marriage, the image of the stallion may have become a Corvette, but we truly believed that our perfect prince was out there complete with the perfect wedding. And what beautiful and exquisite images we had available to fuel our imaginations as we saw weddings that promised everything, from the regal ceremony of Maria to the handsome Captain von Trapp in *The Sound of Music* to the stunning spectacle and grandeur of royal weddings. Our mother's generation had the real-life example of the elegant movie star Grace Kelly and Prince Rainier of Monaco. Most of us witnessed and to some extent lived inside the dream of the marriage of Prince Charles and Lady Diana. Grace Kelly and Diana Spencer were beautiful women with lonely beginnings being saved by wealthy, handsome men who elevated them up to a life of a noble woman. Nothing and no one in our growing-up years cautioned us against the idealism of the fairy-tale model, and even as we were confronted with the real life tragedies of Grace and Diana, it didn't really sway us from wanting to believe in the "happily-ever-after" ending. For what we did not learn from the evidence facing us or previous generations—maybe because they believed it too—was that the happy ending portrayed in the storybooks was nothing more than fluff and fantasy.

Generations of this misconception of what love should be has been passed down to both boys and girls. Nobody questioned what happened after the glowing couple disappeared off the pages of the story. These stereotypical behavior norms and expectations portrayed men as the rescuers and women as needing to be rescued. Why wouldn't they? He rescued her, didn't he? And they got married, didn't they? The story instructed us to believe that marriage was simply a continuation of the fairy tale, a shadowy world were everything was always okay because these two were somehow, magically, perfectly matched (mostly because he was handsome and she was beautiful). Somewhere along the way, we developed the idea that "happily ever after" more or less happened automatically after we got married. Of course the prince and his princess bride never disagreed, or fought, or cried, or stomped out of the house.

But anyone who has had a long-term significant other knows that really, the biggest leap of imagination was that this beautiful couple lived "happily ever after." I remember the sense of betrayal of my dreams when my childhood image of my future married life had been shattered after a failed "fairy-tale" relationship. Nothing about my wedding day, the dreams, the beautiful wedding gown, the gifts, or the presence of friends and family at an exquisite wedding, protected me from that failure.

This is what I call the fairy-tale model of marriage. You meet someone; he "rescues" you and you fall instantly in love, get married, and live that life of infinite happiness. It is a model that is not only in fairly tales. It's in all our entertainment—movies, songs, books. How many of you secretly enjoyed Harlequin Romance novels when you were young or read the prolific romance authors of our day? We long to have someone sing to us the countless love songs on the radio. We flock to see movies such as *Grease, Pretty Woman, An Officer and a Gentleman, You've Got Mail, Sleepless in Seattle* and others like them because the entire entertainment industry has figured out that there's gold in them thar stories. The gold, of course, is nothing more than the pull of romance. Really, where would Hollywood be without it? To the creators of movies, the writers of books, the composers of songs, the tellers of stories, love, indeed, makes the world go 'round—or at least finances the effort. And while *love* is big business, what we have failed to see is the damage that all of this fairy-tale thinking has done to our ideas of what goes into making a good marriage, beyond the dream of the wedding day.

Indeed, around the middle of the last century, as society began to pursue self-expression and it became acceptable to reflect the dating and search process in songs, a detrimental trend began. Take the movie *American Graffiti*. It was a movie made in 1973 about being teenagers in the early 1960s. The songs in it are revealing in that they demonstrate what we've come to think we "want" in a partner. We've been listening to these songs for decades, maybe even generations, and so a closer look at them can be instructive. Most of the songs are about the external qualities that we want our potential mate to possess. The Big Bopper wants "chantilly lace, a pretty face, a pony tail, a wiggle in the walk, a giggle in the talk," [1] another wants a party doll to make love to, and another wants "Love Potion No. 9" to make himself incurably romantic. Even that magnificent song by the Platters, "Only You," misses the point because all the longing they croon into the words: "only you can make this change in me...when you hold my hand, I understand the magic that you do," [2] is not only unrelated to marital success, but in many cases it may actually be detrimental. In fact, this one song exposes much of what is harmful about the fairy-tale myth. The singer laments that he is incomplete and needs to change but lacks the ability or self-discipline to do it himself. He is incapable or unwilling, either because he's too lazy or too ill-equipped to do the hard work necessary himself, and so he decides to rely on the woman of his dreams to do it for him. With a wry grin, we should recognize that this is the reverse fairy tale, where she gets to "rescue" him.

So, in all these type of songs, we see the lie of the fairy tale. The eventual objective for many of these romantic advances is either possession of the man or woman or the "event" itself, the marriage ceremony. Rarely do these songs mention that marriage is a beginning, not an ending. While the courtship leading to marriage is full of romance, aching expectation, and a whole lot 'o fun, what happens after the ceremony is entirely ignored. Unfortunately, many of us seem to approach the marriage ceremony as the goal rather than seeing it as commencement. Contrast this with the step in school where you graduate. Academia gets it right when they call graduation a "commencement," a beginning, because what is important is not that one has graduated but what one does with their acquired knowledge in the next fifty or more years.

Now before we go any further, let me not diminish the importance of love and romance. The Bible underlines the importance of love by using the word more than six hundred times, often in the romantic sense. Good strong marriages are full of love and romance; as I said in the preface, I want my own marriage to be the romance of the century. Disappointingly, however, we know that the intense pleasure associated with love and romance is often matched and exceeded by the disaster of divorce, the scourge of separation, the cancer of criticism, the bayonet of betrayal, the affliction of abuse, the lament of loneliness, or even the banality of boredom. We have all seen or experienced first-hand enough challenged or broken relationships (and the resulting devastation) to realize that love is not without price, and we wonder, "Is it possible to experience the love without the trauma?"

Many of us have spent our lifetime wishing, hoping against all hope, that we really will find our Prince Charming. We want the Hollywood ending, and while I firmly believe that "happily ever after" is possible, it is the way that we've gone about finding our Prince Charming that is the trouble. We stay so focused on the emotions of the fairy tale, that it's likely that we missed the real culprit to our problem. We fall in love and *then* attempt to determine if he's right. The ideal is to *first* establish what we should be looking for and then let the emotion develop after we found someone who at least initially fits the bill. The violation of this ideal has created heaps of trouble because we have used emotion, fueled by books and movies, as a guide to tell us what to look for in a mate, how to search or wait for a mate, and horrors, what to expect in a marriage. No doubt everyone seeks success in their marriage, but they too often start with the wrong blue print, model, or set of rules, and their search for knowledge finds them studying in the wrong library or hunting in the wrong forest. They are like the ancient alchemists seeking to find gold in worthless rocks. No matter how sincere your efforts to gain success, if your model or source of information about what is "right" is flawed, the eventual result will be equally flawed.

So, let's start the deconstruction process and look at what's wrong with our current ideas about marriage and then reconstruct in the next chapter what goes into making a superlative marriage. Based on the fairy-tale model, there are two foundational reasons why we choose marriage partners who aren't right for us:

1. We're ignorant of principles that govern marital success, and
2. Strong emotions overwhelm sound judgment.

PRINCIPLES THAT GOVERN MARITAL SUCCESS ARE UNKNOWN

People searching for a partner can be ignorant in many ways. For instance, we may think that we know what we're doing but more often than not, we don't. It's really nothing more than a case of being blind but thinking you are sighted. When we're young for instance, this manifests itself by thinking that Prince Charming is the studliest hunk. Our assessment of a good relationship is based solely on physical appearance, but in reality you soon learn that getting married because your potential husband is a hottie gives you little chance of producing a successful marriage. As we mature we recognize that a marriage is based on more than physical appearance, but unknowingly still use limited or incorrect criteria. Once you have either gone through a failed relationship or a failed marriage has burned you, you often begin a new search thinking you understand the reasons for your past relationship's failure. These interpretations and reasons are typically flawed, but you forge unknowingly ahead and usually select someone with mismatches or problems similar to your first failed attempt. In other words, the man looks different, but the problems are relatively the same.

Another path of ignorance is followed by people who are at least aware that they lack knowledge, but are ignorant of success principles and often don't know where to turn for help. The bewildered searcher rightly laments, "What should I do?" "How can I know?" "Is this the right one?" They know that they don't know, but have not been able to access—up to this point—the appropriate knowledge or advice. They may even be suspicious of qualified help if they had used a counselor at the end of a failing marriage, becoming distrustful because it failed anyway.

SOUND JUDGMENT IS OVERWHELMED

The second foundational reason why we choose marriage partners who aren't right for us occurs when sound judgment is overwhelmed by the tide of emotion. Have you ever been so drowned in emotion that you can't think straight? How often have you seen dating couples who break up, get back together, break up, get back together; and all the world screams "Wake up, don't you know that he's completely wrong for you?" Or maybe you have seen people make dreadful relationship choices because of sexual or emotional entanglement. Perhaps they had an intense need for comfort, nurturance, or validation because they were lonely, in pain, or feeling trapped? Do you have a friend that picked a mate because she just gave up and decided that a known but inferior relationship was better than none?

Let us revisit the fairy tale and examine the role of emotion. Two important questions arise. First, does initial infatuation predict marital success? Research provides a simple (but unpopular) answer. "Very rarely." [3] Second, does the fairy-tale model or myth still represent present attitudes toward romance and marriage? Recent research not only says yes, but actually indicates that people today attach even greater importance to being "in love" as a prerequisite for marriage than they did in the past few decades. [4]

So, let's look for a moment at the consequences of this fairy-tale model. In North America we experience a 50 percent divorce rate of first marriages, a 60 percent divorce rate of second and subsequent marriages, with an even higher percentage of failure when blended families are involved. [5] These cold statistics reflect months, and in many cases, years of agony and disrupted lives. If a divorce involves children, the disputes and unhappiness might go on for up to twenty years as former partners wrangle over matters of custody, visitation, and child support. Beyond the 50-60 percent divorce rate, there are many who stay in a relationship because of religious principles, "because of the kids," or for financial or other reasons. All love has ended; they sleep in separate beds, and a sense of isolation and loneliness, antagonism or a cool hostility pervades the atmosphere. Research suggests that only about 20 percent of marriages might be considered successful, and only 7 percent are exceptional.[6]

My point is that many marriages are challenged because they are built on the unsound principles of the fairy-tale model. A wealth of research has explored the issue of successful and unsuccessful marriages and an awareness of these findings will equip you with the knowledge necessary to make a wiser choice. To illustrate, let's compare the findings of research psychology with the personal qualities of our fairy-tale princess and explore the likelihood of the success of her relationship with Prince Charming.

Physical Attractiveness: First, our princess in the stories or in the movies is almost always beautiful. Research finds that while most people enjoy and value beauty, very beautiful people are typically not as successful in marriages as their less fetching peers.[7] Most of their lives, the factor of beauty has heavily assisted them with making friends and easily attracting the opposite sex rather than learning and using good relationship skills. Their beauty also has provided them easy access to additional suitors when a romance fails. For example, observe the marital record of some of the ultra beautiful in the entertainment industry. While there have been some marriages that lasted a lifetime, most notably Jimmy Stewart or Fred Astair,* these are more than overwhelmed by examples such as Elizabeth Taylor (8 marriages), Rex Harrison (6), Betty Davis (5), Judy Garland (5), and Cary Grant (5). [*Astair actually married a second time following the death of his first wife.]

Charm and Adornment: Second, there's the focus on how Prince Charming dresses and on how, well, charming he is. We all like someone who dresses well, but Carly Simon's delicious song, "You're so Vain," reminds us to beware of someone who merely looks good: "You walked into the party like you were walking onto a yacht, your hat strategically dipped below one eye, your scarf it was apricot...And all the girls dreamed that they'd be your partner....But you gave away the things you loved, and one of them was me." [8] Essentially anyone can put on an attractive exterior, and plenty of "wolves" come across as being some of the most appealing men you'll ever meet. I can't tell you how many women have told me how they were "charmed off their feet" by the typical "player" who knows all the right phrases, buys all the right presents, and just does all the right things. But, that Prince Charming quickly shows his true colors when things get even the tiniest bit serious. Research confirms that marital success is not associated with external adornment or charm.[9]

Intoxicating Emotions: Third, we look at the intensity of emotional arousal and passion suggested by all the pop songs and current movie renditions of the fairy-tale model. Long ago, psychological research uncovered one central truth about emotions: they fluctuate.[10] A high, one moment is followed by a low the next. Intense passion (interpreted as romantic love) in the face of betrayal, or worse, abuse can easily shift to equally intense hatred and loathing. In short, romantic passion tends to blind rather than to clarify your thoughts in the search for a successful relationship.[11]

Premature Sense of Ownership: If you listen closely to the lyrics of many love songs, you hear over and over such things as, "she's my baby, she's my pet," or "she's mine." Our fairy tale emphasizes that Prince Charming will rescue and take care of us, but often the related human emotion on his part is that we now belong to him body and soul. The typical response of our hero in today's songs and movies (largely based on this premature sense of ownership) is to defend his love, downplay the negatives, build up the positives, and continue to deceive himself into the mistaken belief that serious issues are unimportant. Not only will this be a source of communication problems, it also may yield controlling behaviors on his part. We might be attracted initially to this "strong man" persona, but once again, according to research, we should continue our search. In context of dating, where a relationship has not stood the test of time, the premature sense of ownership has great capacity to distort one's ability to determine a good fit.[12]

Instant Romance: "We fell in love on the night we met," is the backbone of the fairy-tale model. And although we love to believe in the idea of "love at first sight," psychology has found that in "instant" romances in which a marriage occurs within thirty days of the initial contact there is an astonishing 95 percent failure rate.[13] While there are a fair number of successful marriages that eventually grow out of a first-love experience, the impulsive early marriage, arising out of an initial attraction, almost always fails.

Youth: How old were you when you first said, "I do!" What kind of pressure did you feel from your friends, peers, graduation schedule, or internal time clock? We wanted to be the princess, with her beautiful wedding, and her flawless figure and skin. What did we know about life? In the early 1960s Johnny Burnette recorded the smash hit song with the lyrics, "You're sixteen, you're beautiful, and you're mine." [14] But what resources does a sixteen year old have to make choices that have such an enormous impact on life happiness? A hard, cold look at teen marriages reveals up to a 90 percent failure rate. [15] Okay, so maybe you weren't sixteen when you married, but it's likely that most of your relational savvy came from personal experience or advice from your friends. And the scary question is how much of that youthful perspective and search process are you still inadvertently using today? After all, these are the default settings taught to us by stories in early childhood.

Illusion: My final thought is not as research-based, but it has surfaced enough in my counseling that I want to address it here. In recent years, Hollywood has taken Prince Charming one deceitful step further. The most attractive men seem in some way "bad boys," the quintessential "players." As Hollywood introduced these players, it encouraged an insidious acceptance of them and their behavior. It began with Rhett Butler in *Gone with the Wind*. In spite of his checkered past, his reputation of womanizing, and his association with a brothel, we came to accept Rhett because we knew he loved Scarlett with amazing passion. We then agreed that he was worth having, and by the end of the movie, we too were in love with Rhett. It continues today with James Bond who routinely seduces and discards his lovers. He couldn't stay with one woman longer than the length of a cruise if his life depended on it (and yes, he did get married once but Mrs. Bond was conveniently offed soon after the wedding). As we watch these magnificent specimens of masculinity, we sigh at their remarkable prowess, but need to see that they are rotten marriage material. Just as Hollywood helped make the fairy-tale model acceptable to all of us, it elevated a player so that not only was he palatable but actually admired. We forget that the illusion of such men is a delusion of reality. Truly, that a "bad boy" will make a good husband is as unbelievable as Barbie's anatomically incorrect dimensions! Players simply don't make good marriage partners, and Barbie can't walk.

The verdict of the analysis by psychological research is that the relationships that are based on the fairy-tale model have less than a one in a hundred chance of survival. Now, don't get me wrong. In no way do I want to criticize the various components of relationships: sex, beauty, passion, charm, impulse. They're all part of life, make for great stories, and play their appropriate role in human experience. But if you want a wonderful marriage that lasts a lifetime, let's throw away the fairy tale and look at what is real. Now, just to be fair, Hollywood is starting to see the error of its ways. The hit movie, *Shrek*, is a fairy tale that brilliantly deconstructs the fairy-tale model. The princess Fiona is not thin and beautiful, but she definitely knows what she wants. Prince Charming is a spoiled, nasty man, and the true "Mr. Right" is an ogre: overweight, uncouth, and a bit unkempt—definitely not handsome. But, he too, knows that his "princess" is exactly what he needs and wants in a mate. Their romance flourishes because they have what it takes to make a good relationship, the same interests and values. A wonderful, successful marriage requires you do your homework first. So, let's take our cure *and* our courage from Fiona and Shrek. It is likely that your Prince Charming is out there. He is real, but you have to figure out what "real" is to you before you can hunt in the right forest and set out in search of him.

Chapter 2

WHAT DOES "HAPPILY EVER AFTER" *REALLY* LOOK LIKE?

The Ideal Marriage

O kay, so I may have just totally dismantled one of your most cherished ideas. Or perhaps you experienced one of those "aha" moments of insight. But, just because the marriage in the fairy tale doesn't ever get talked about, it doesn't mean that you can't have a wonderful, fulfilling marriage that some would still call "fairy tale." Happily ever after *is* possible and if you look hard enough, you will find marvelous examples of successful marriages. But because they are not the "norm," discovering what characteristics make up those marriages is of great interest. We now turn to examining the model of those marriages.

As I told you in the preface of the book, I am a counselor. My background is in human resource management and small business counseling which incorporates a great deal of psychology and sociology. Working with small business owners over the past twenty years, I was struck by how often the health of someone's marriage had a remarkable impact on the success of their business. This awareness was added to the information collected during my own deep search for knowledge about the best way to go about the process of healing and then finding a mate. I had not yet met my husband, Darren, and as I was doing my own research, I became increasingly interested in helping people in the midst of marital issues and in the process was certified in a Seminary-based Lay Counseling training program. Darren, whom I met on the Internet (match.com), is a psychologist, and has a Ph.D. from UCLA (he's the research brain in this endeavor). Like me, he was very interested in healing others in their marital difficulties. Very early on in our "getting to know each other" phase, he shared with me that he had put together a dating model. The material that I explore in this chapter originates from his research, our own application of his model, and the seminars we subsequently created to help people find and enter into a fulfilling marriage that will last a lifetime.

One of the first issues that we have to address is the fact that most women have limited role models for what a good marriage looks like. Excellent relationships are out there, but they are hard to find. As I cited in the last chapter, all in all, only about 20 percent of marriages might be considered successful, and according to therapist Gregory Popcak, only 7 percent are exceptional.[1] If you're forty or older, you probably have a mother who wasn't brought up in our modern age of women's liberation. She grew up in the forties or earlier and was raised to believe that her needs and wants were secondary and subordinate to her family's or her husband's. And in the event that her marriage didn't turn out to be the fairy tale of her dreams, the culture she was in mandated that she accept her circumstances. While the divorce rate itself was lower due to cultural unacceptability, the health of marriages was often poor with the women living in silent despair.

So, the first question that you should be asking yourself in your quest for Mr. Right is not about the man himself, but what does a good, strong, loving marriage look like. Without a clear picture of the components of a successful marriage, we don't know what we're looking for, either in a man or in a marriage. In the battlefield left after years of a 50 percent divorce rate, we rarely encounter a couple experiencing an excellent marriage. Fortunately, among the strong marriages that do exist, research has pinpointed areas that make them successful. My hope is that as I construct for you a portrait of what a good marriage truly looks like, you will be better able to negotiate the path to success in this, the most complicated of all human relationships.

From research, I have organized ten different critical areas into three categories. As you read what they are, know that each of the ten allows considerable latitude for a particular couple to create the dynamics of their own marriage, but, in successful marriages all ten areas are present.

As you read through them, if possible envision instances where you've seen these present in your relationship or in others' as well. It is likely that you have seen most of them, just not necessarily combined into one marriage:

♥ **The Friendship Dynamic**
  - Friendship and mutual interests
  - Shared passionate goals

♥ **The Romantic Love Dynamic**
  - Love and romance
  - Traditions and shared meaning
  - Encouragement and gratitude

♥ **The Foundations of Successful Marriage**
  - Shared spiritual or philosophical perspective
  - Communication and conflict-resolution skills
  - Commitment
  - Family
  - Procedures in place for continued growth

The order of the three main categories is designed to show the progression of a successful relationship. From friendship develops romantic love. When the romance progresses to a certain stage, then the couple considers issues that provide a secure foundation for long-term success.

THE FRIENDSHIP DYNAMIC

Friendship and Mutual Interests

℞

Friendship and mutual interests are combined into one category because friendships typically grow out of mutual interests. A musician's closest friends are usually other musicians, and the same goes for football fans, academics, business people, politicians, entertainers, and even serious stamp collectors. By contrast, romance so often begins with the powerful chemistry of sexual attraction that the idea of shared interests, even friendship, is ignored. My husband remembers a math teacher he worked with at a high school in California. He was an excellent teacher and an even better football coach. At that time, he was in his late thirties and divorced. Shortly after my husband began teaching at the high school, the coach married an attractive Hispanic girl and daily glowed with pleasure. A year later, however, the glow had disappeared; he confided that he and his wife had absolutely nothing in common and lived what is called parallel lives. He had his interests; she had hers, and their life paths did not cross. It was almost as if their house was a hotel where they came and went independently of each other.

One of the questions that I often ask dating couples is: "If your partner was the same sex as you and there was no romantic component to the relationship, would you still be good friends?" Some people respond that all they want to do is "be" with that person, that they like doing the mundane things of life together like washing dishes, doing laundry, or watching TV. Such a response should raise concern. You don't want to say when it's all over, "My husband and I washed 598,000 dishes, completed 37,000 loads of laundry, and watched 517,000 hours of mindless TV, but we did it together." You want your relationship to encourage and challenge you to learn, to grow, to contribute, to become better in ways that make a difference to those you touch. If all you share is the occasional movie and a couple of TV programs, it is unlikely that a rich integrated relationship, and a good marriage, will result. Shared vocational, financial, personal, artistic, aesthetic, or spiritual interests provide greater substance to your lives, and they enhance the quality of your marriage.

℞ *Shared Passionate Mission, Vision, and/or Goals*

Famed psychologist Nathaniel Brandon states that the most powerful predictor of individual self-esteem is progressive attainment of meaningful goals.[2] Similarly, one of the greatest predictors of successful marriage is the mutual pursuit of shared goals.[3] Even outside of marriage, some of the strongest friendships are secured by individuals who work together to accomplish similar objectives: an athlete working with teammates in pursuit of a championship; the business partners laboring together to build financial success; the community workers building a more beautiful neighborhood. When shared goals are mutually pursued, the fabric of any relationship is enriched. This is as true for marriage as it is for any partnership. If a common goal can bring even enemies together (observe the alliance of the U.S. and Britain with the Soviet Union to counter the threat of Hitler) how much more will it strengthen the bonds of friendship and marriage?

These goals may encompass almost infinite variety. You both may want to be worth a million bucks by age forty, or you would like to publish a co-authored best seller. You both may have similar goals in the area of personal qualities like greater compassion, spirituality, and integrity. Perhaps you both want to climb the ten tallest peaks in the world, visit the ten greatest art museums, or raise millions to provide safe drinking water for residents of third-world countries. The goals themselves are limited only by what your fertile brain may concoct; the most important point is that you create them together.

When you are pursuing your goals together, something wonderful called synergy frequently emerges. Synergy is the quality of two or more people that allows them to accomplish more as a result of being together than they could do separately. Nikken Corporation independent consultants and million-dollar earners Bob and Trish Schwenkler have synergy. Trish is the hyperactive go-getter, while Bob provides the vital support function maintaining the communication centers, the family patterns, and the financial records that allow Trish to go out and do what she does best. It is unlikely that such extraordinary business success could have happened if each had been working independently. While a couple will never have synergy in all areas of their lives, the greater the number of areas of productive interactive accomplishment, the more vibrant will be their relationship.

The Romantic Love Dynamic

Nurturing Love and Romance   ℞

When we first meet our potential mate, we want to be in love. We want to experience that breathless urgency, that aching desire. Psychologist Dorothy Tennov conducted long-range research on the in-love experience and finds that this "romantic obsession" lasts an average of about two years.[4] While most marriages start out in the rosy glow of being in love, what happens to love when the two years is completed?

In an excellent relationship, real love emerges from the initial in-love stage. Erich Fromm calls this the love of choice and discipline. He states that it is something that must be "worked at" in order to flourish.[5] Real love is the stuff of which successful marriages are made. It initiates action, seeks growth in one's self and one's partner, and although it emanates from our choices, the consequences of those choices are rich emotions and powerful bonds of unity. The key to a successful transition from being in love to real love centers in the concept of "romantic acts." Romantic acts are actions performed to help one's beloved feel treasured. These romantic acts exist in profusion during the in-love phase, but as one moves beyond that high, a different dynamic emerges. In real love you continue to do the romantic acts even if you may not feel like it.

The simple reality is that emotions are a response to action. If you do the acts, romance will flourish within the context of daily living: the warm touch, the occasional flowers, frequent love notes, poems, the joke, the smile, the chuckle, the many different reminders that your partner is special. These acts keep the flame alive. The teenage-style passion will occur from time to time as opportunity (or plans) allow. And that passion can be enhanced by the months and years that love has been nurtured. Kisses sweeter than fine aged wine can be the reality for many decades in the good marriage. Because the understanding of the nature of love, how and when we experience it, and how it influences our judgment is so important, I am going to delve further into it in the next chapter. But, for now, I will continue on with painting my picture of the ideal marriage for you in broad strokes.

R̸ *Traditions and Shared Meaning*

A good marriage also is one where traditions and shared meaning are developed over time. These shared traditions bring a specialness and uniqueness to a marriage and help pull the entire family together. Over time, couples develop rituals. Special meanings get attached to meals, holidays, religious activities, celebrations, methods of relaxation, and many others. If you come from an Italian background, for example, you generally will have some sort of pasta at all holiday meals. Your husband could come to truly enjoy that particular addition to the usual fair of turkey or ham or roast, and your children will participate in these traditions. I have found that my girls have even helped create new traditions and rituals that become family favorites.

Traditions may stem from your own past experiences, your present concerns and activities, or from future aspirations, but they don't all need to be complex or elaborate. My husband and I have a Thursday night date in which we pop corn, snuggle down, watch a video, and elbow each other as we fight over the last kernels in the bowl. We exert zealous efforts to make certain that our Thursday nights aren't booked with other events.

Outstanding marriages are typically rich in traditions that nurture the mystery and wonder of life. And, know that every time you participate in a tradition you are saying, "I love you!" in a distinctive way.

Encouragement and Gratitude   ℞

Criticism withers the bones; gratitude and encouragement nourish the spirit. A good marriage avoids criticism. I typically call criticism "the cheapest form of human emission." The greatest men and women in politics, science, entertainment, and athletics are often harshly criticized by people who have never achieved their level of success, have no concept of the challenges they face, and possess only a fraction of their talent or intelligence. Rather than being a faultfinder, be a good-finder. Express gratitude to your partner, encourage your partner, lavishly, unstintingly, frequently. Never take each other for granted. In so doing, you will, indeed, nourish the spirit and make glad the heart. A story illustrates:

> Some time ago at the University of Wisconsin there were twenty young men who were outstanding writers. These men were articulate word merchants and everyone expected great things from them. They formed a club that met monthly to read and comment on each other's works. At first they would make useful critiques, but soon they started to move toward criticism and eventually the conversation in those meetings could only be described as downright vicious. They named themselves "The Stranglers." Also at that time, there were a number of women at the University of Wisconsin who were also very talented writers. They decided to form a club for the same purpose as the men. But their atmosphere was quite different. They would complement each other for the things they had written, encourage each other, and any suggestions would be given constructively. Well, thirty years later, none of the twenty men had accomplished anything as an author, but six of the women rose to national prominence including Marjorie Kinnan Rawlings who wrote *The Yearling*. As I listen to the conversations around me, the scripts of TV shows, the format of news reports etc. I find that we have become experts at criticism. So, at the risk of pounding this point into the ground, please consider another example. Again it has to do with a writing group, this one called the Inklings, which met at Cambridge in the 1940s and 1950s. Consider that a marriage is like a group; if

you criticize, nothing is produced and failure results. But when you encourage, great work emerges. In this case, the Inklings produced the two best selling authors of the twentieth century: J.R.R. Tolkien with his *Lord of the Rings* trilogy and C.S. Lewis who wrote many best sellers including *The Chronicles of Narnia*.

Gratitude is being thankful, expressing gratitude is as simple as letting your spouse know what you appreciate. Whether it's his actions or his attitudes, you need to thank him for what pleases you as well as for doing things you would rather not look after yourself. For example, I am very thankful when Darren either mentors or disciplines the children when there's a subject that's too painful or too difficult for me to handle. I am not only extremely grateful for his participation, but I also I let him know it. The opposite of gratitude is assumption; it assumes that your partner recognizes what pleases you and what doesn't, and what makes you feel special or shares and/or relieves you of your burdens. In other words, if you don't express your gratitude, then you run the risk of taking your partner for granted, and *no one* likes to be taken for granted. Gratitude also has another wonderful side effect.

Prominent marital expert, John Gottman, has discovered that excellent relationships maintain a 5:1 (or higher) ratio of positive to negative interactions, suggesting that five times as much attention should be devoted to encouragement and gratitude as is given to criticism and assumption.[6] Success in all relationships is accompanied by encouragement, including marriage. And when you express gratitude for your spouse and his thoughtfulness—by not taking him for granted—it sets the stage for your marriage to flourish.

THE FOUNDATIONS FOR LONG-TERM SUCCESS

℞ *Shared Spiritual or Philosophical Perspectives*

If a business is to operate successfully, it must have a common mission. Both the administration and workers share the business's values and goals and agree to work toward achieving them. If a country is to flourish, it must have an agreed-upon constitution that supplies the structure and procedures to provide for the needs of the citizens and conduct the business of government. In a marriage, the same applies.

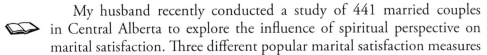 My husband recently conducted a study of 441 married couples in Central Alberta to explore the influence of spiritual perspective on marital satisfaction. Three different popular marital satisfaction measures

were used in this survey, and the results were indisputable for all three measures: 1) those with similar spiritual perspective had greater marital satisfaction; 2) those from the same religious group or denomination had greater marital satisfaction; and 3) those who scored higher on overall spirituality had the happiest marriages.

Good marriages consist of both partners having similar philosophies, and this includes shared spiritual beliefs. If a couple is atheist, they need to agree on the values they both espouse. If both are highly spiritual, the same discussion of values is necessary. Good marriages are made when both parties have similar purpose, meaning, and basic philosophy of life.

When marriages used to be arranged, spiritual compatibility was not as much of an issue. You married the man your family selected, and they chose him because he operated under their own belief structure. However, once arranged marriages gave way to "love matches," the challenge of spiritual compatibility emerged. It is important that I say this again: it doesn't matter so much what a person's spiritual beliefs are. What does matter is that both partners mesh in their spiritual perspective.

Communication and Conflict-Resolution Skills
℞

Garrison Keillor, on his famous *A Prairie Home Companion* radio program, once told a story about a couple who was having trouble. The daughter's father, concerned about what was going on, asked his grown child how her marriage was going. She told her father that she and her husband were working on it. Keillor, in his humble wisdom, then had the father ruminate on the fact that all marriages are continually "working on it." [7] It's not easy to put two people together who have individual wants and needs. Fate is a myth, and the truth is, a good marriage really is one that is continually "working on it." Part of working on it is the development of excellent communication and conflict-resolution skills.

Within the context of any relationship, there are two broad categories of communication: 1) pleasant, enjoyable, nurturing forms of interaction that nourish the soul and add to life's pleasure, and 2) conflict-resolution skills, (or negotiating skills) that allow you to resolve differences of opinion. Remember the Gottman ratio of 5:1? Just like with criticism and gratitude, five times as much attention should be devoted to the positive aspects of communication as is devoted to the negative.

℞ However, differences of opinion are an absolute staple of any marriage, whether we like it or not. The ability to resolve those differences is therefore critical to the success of any relationship. While the phrase "conflict resolution" may arouse bad memories, do realize that for couples skilled at resolving differences, the sheer number of conflicts is minimized and damaging escalation is largely eliminated. And fortunately, it is a skill, something that you can make a choice to learn. Healthy marriages have some sort of conflict resolution plan in place with the couple willing and able to use it when conflict erupts. You can imagine my surprise when, on our honeymoon trip on the train from Alabama to Alberta, Darren got out a piece of paper and casually suggested that we work on a conflict-resolution plan. My first reaction was "*Ick*. This isn't a romance topic for a honeymoon." But, as he gently persevered in sharing its importance, we outlined a half page with stages, steps, and bullet points on our personal process. Now, when I think back to our honeymoon, in one of those peculiar tricks that memory plays on us, I can hear the clickety-clack of the train and still feel the almost tangible love that shimmered between us as we created an insurance plan for our future.

℞ *Commitment*

Commitment has gotten a bad rap over the years. Perhaps a contributor to this is that there were many of us who grew up with parents who maintained a clench-your-fists, grit-your-teeth sort of commitment in an empty relationship. That is not the stuff of good marriages. Real commitment is of much richer substance. It, of course, includes sexual and personal fidelity, but that is only a beginning.

Ideally the greater part of commitment is primarily found in the positive things that we do rather than just the negative things that we avoid. Commitment, in a way, is the keystone to all good marriages and it encompasses everything that we will talk about in this book: continued romantic acts, knowing your partner, communication skills, learning his or her various languages, expressions of gratitude.

I know one couple, Albert and Ginny, who are wonderfully committed to each other. Albert, in conversation with others, speaks glowingly about the wonderful qualities of his wife, Ginny, and he makes a point of doing it when she is within hearing range! This is an expression of commitment that supports the relationship in a most wonderful way. In the excellent marriage, commitment becomes part of the foundation that cannot be shaken by the occasional squabble or disagreement. It becomes the bedrock of security that helps the couple weather life's storms.

Family

R_X

While the idea of "family" has a myriad of different meanings and is predicated on some intensely personal criteria, the fact of the matter is that when you marry, you create a "family." There are a number of different definitions of family, and psychology provides perhaps the most useful definition: "Any group of persons united by the ties of marriage, blood, or adoption, or any sexually expressive relationship in which 1) the people are committed to one another in an intimate, interpersonal relationship; 2) the members see their identity as importantly attached to the group; and 3) the group has an identity of its own."

Based on this definition, the key components of family, then, appear to be "intimate interpersonal relationships," "fellowship," and "group identity." How the tapestry of these and other components are woven together, how the symphony is composed, will be as diverse as the couples who attempt it. However it may be shaped, the importance of the idea of "family" is never diminished in a good marriage. In discussions between the two of you, the nature of *your* family can be explored in all its richness. It is the entity that follows from having a strong commitment, for when two people pledge to spending the rest of their lives together, they commit to creating themselves as a "family." And this is something that is very, very powerful indeed.

Procedures in Place for Continued Growth

R_X

As I said in the communication section, all good marriages are committed to "working on it," and there is no more powerful way to "work" on a strong marriage than to put into place activities and procedures that will promote a couple's continued growth together. Think of those who are exceptionally good in any field. What are the qualities or activities that result in outstanding performance? Typically it is a combination of innate talent, thousands of hours acquiring appropriate knowledge, and skillful application of that knowledge. In relationships, we may have little control over our initial "talent level." What we *do* have control over is the acquisition and application of knowledge.

A good marriage is one where both partners devote a portion of each day or week to learn more about each other and more about ways to enhance the relationship. A weak marriage emerges when the partners quit learning about each other. When this occurs, the partners no longer have the resources or the motivation for continued growth. The result is that the vibrancy of their relationship begins to wane. My husband and I spend time daily (typically about ten minutes) reading and applying material from good books on relationships. We have found that it provides a continual flow of new ideas and useful insights, and we plan to continue this process for a lifetime.

A Final Word

So there you have it, a full picture of what a good marriage consists of. Its component parts sometimes do not seem very romantic, but when a couple has all of these aspects in place in some way or another, the romance automatically follows. If you have shared interests, goals and ideals, when you are communicating and "working" on your marriage, you are creating it together, so that when the first blush of love wanes, the strong, true, passion of real love can emerge and grow. This portrait is what I ultimately want for everyone who reads this book. But before we begin to delve into the pre*fix* process, we need to take up the subject of *real love* as the last lesson in Marriage 101. As I pointed out earlier, understanding the nature love, how and when we experience it, and how it influences our judgment is crucial to preparing for a successful marriage.

* Chapter 3 *

What's Love Got to Do with It?

Unraveling the Mysteries of "A Many-Splendored Thing"

We love to be in love, don't we? Our world celebrates the magnificence of romantic love, and I'm the first one to say that love is vital to any relationship. It is grand to be in love, to feel the intensity of its passion. But why is it that I've had so many women either divorced or on the verge, tell me they thought they really would live "happily ever after" because they had such intense feelings for their mate?

The problem with love is most people misunderstand the role it plays in their relationship. We have been inundated with all sorts of messages, both overt and covert, that celebrate the intensity of emotion that certain stages of love bring. Because our culture says it's okay to date over and over again, we have become conditioned to seek out the intense emotion that comes with the first stages of love. But we incorrectly think that the intensity of our feeling is the criteria we should use to judge if the relationship is good or not. In fact, love is often held as the preeminent criteria, and because of that, we incorrectly monitor the health of our relationship based on the intensity of our emotional love for the other person.

But you see, feeling love isn't the problem. It's how we have applied our understanding of that feeling that is the problem. Because love's role in the whole process of developing and maintaining a relationship is misunderstood, I'm devoting this chapter to help you understand the natural development of stages toward love, to show you where misconceptions lie, and to disabuse you of the idea that when the intensity of the in-love state wanes, something is wrong. It is of paramount importance that you understand this concept.

The premise of the fairy-tale model, that we meet, fall instantly in love, get married and live forever happy has caused us to misapply the interpretation of love to the whole dating process. It has conditioned us into our current path of developing feelings first and then trying to determine if he is the right fit. In its simplest terms, that's putting the cart before the horse. Love is a major contributor to a healthy marriage, but it's just not the first step. The entire thrust of this book is to help you first apply some thought and criteria in your search process and then allow your feelings to blossom. So let's celebrate love as magnificent and important, but let's eradicate the myth that your degree of love is a measure of the health or the rightness of your relationship.

You need to have a better understanding of the stages of love so that you know what role it really plays in the courtship process and in the relationship as a whole. In order to have a healthy long-term relationship, you must be armed with the knowledge of where the different stages of love emerge, and how unreliable love is as a measure of compatibility. Our current *modus operandi* is love first, ask questions later, but the reason why that's not a reliable indicator is because love evolves and changes throughout the course of a relationship. Love should not be the leading element in your decision making process; rather it should arise out of all the other indicators of compatibility—the ones that you get to discover in the rest of the book.

The type of love that will last a lifetime is dependant on successfully navigating the changing waters of love as it moves from infatuation, through the intensity of the in-love state, to the desired long-range goal of having the choice of real love. If you don't know what real love is yet, don't worry. You will by the end of this chapter. And consider something else. Once we understand love's proper place in a relationship and recognize which stages it goes through, then we're free to enjoy, savor, and experience it, but never rely on it. Being in love is grand, but it is visceral, arising from instinct rather than reason. It also vacillates, swinging indecisively back and forth. So let's be clear, the presence of love in a relationship is necessary and can be experienced fully, but it is in no way dependable as the leading criteria of compatibility.

LOVE CONQUERS ALL—NOT!

Most of us have experienced the power of being in love. Because of the strength of that feeling and a culture that encourages it, we often believe that love triumphs over all. This is one of the last two century's great fallacies. At our Friday night collegiate group meetings, this point creates great contention. Questions and statements are presented such as: "What about unconditional love, such as what the Bible presents?" or "If we love one another enough, there isn't anything we can't overcome." The simple reality is that the romantic variety of love—the type that is being considered here—will not overcome the differences caused by serious incompatibility. Whether you are hoping, wishing, or even desperately in love, some relationships simply cannot work. For our students, who have attended our group meetings and attend a local Christian university, the difficulty is accentuated because they feel that their faith and prayer life will help their feelings of love overcome any future problems. Darren and I quietly respond that studies show that the divorce rate has increased within the church community as well and in some instances is equivalent to the national rate and is a subject of major concern among church leaders. The point we make is that regardless of church or non-church affiliation, we are focused on reducing the number and degree of challenges *prior* to entering a relationship. The tragedy of incompatibility is that it does not respect one's emotions, beliefs or life practices; it is an equal opportunity marriage destroyer. So if romantic love isn't a sword that conquers all, what is it?

There are actually three phases of love that we need to look at: infatuation, the in-love state, and real love. The first two are the trouble makers; the last is the kind of love that the story books really should be talking about but don't because it doesn't make for exciting story-telling. (It does, however, make for happy marriages, and that's more important, isn't it?) Part of the lure of the first two kinds of love is that it really supports everyone's favorite theme: overcoming impossible odds.

Hollywood gets great mileage out of films that portray people surviving the impossible.

Take James Bond. Even though I bashed him earlier as a "player," I'm a died-in-the-wool Bond fan; he's suave, sexy, witty, and oh so elusive. But, not only does he physically survive impossibly dangerous situations—ones that would kill any mortal human—he also represents the lie of surviving an impossible attraction. The scenario is practically a cliché. He's attracted to some luscious babe and very easily makes his conquest. The women are willing because they are infatuated, but they're surprised when it's left at a one-night stand. They're so overwhelmed with his approach they succumb, thinking that they're going to be the "different one," the one that survives longer than a night. But, no matter how intense their initial attraction, how intensely they feel, it's not going to be reciprocated. Their love can't conquer 007. Let's face it; James Bond is the poster boy for "love-em and leave-em."

Closer to the point is the film *I.Q.* in which a garage mechanic, played by Tim Robbins, attempts to woo a Ph.D. physicist, played by Meg Ryan, who happens to be the niece of Albert Einstein. Quoting Janet Maslin in a 1994 Film Review:

> Oozing total sexual confidence…a mechanic who really likes comets, and…a scientist who doesn't much like auto mechanics… meet, and fall instantly in love. The point, alarmingly, is that brains aren't everything. *I.Q.* is poised to announce that the heart matters more than the head, and that romance is such an equalizer it puts the theory of relativity on an equal footing with fixing cars.[1]

In the movie, love conquers the overpowering reality that one partner is incapable of comprehending what the other is passionate about. His background is so foreign and unrelated to hers that he has to memorize concepts and speeches written by others in her scientific field in order to "speak her language." That's a love that "survives the impossible," but in real life, attempting to make an impossible relationship succeed, regardless of how intense the emotions, is a formula for personal disaster. So if you can't trust the intensity of your feelings, then what can you trust?

The answer, revealed in the pages that follow, is that there is a difference between the passion of infatuation, the passion of the in-love condition, and the passion of mature or real love, and it's vital to the future success of your relationships to recognize these differences. We'll start with infatuation.

INFATUATION

℞

Robert Sternberg, in his Triarchic Theory of Romantic Love defines infatuation as passion without intimacy or commitment.[2] Wikipedia describes it as a "state of being completely carried away by unreasoning passion or love; addictive love…characterized by urgency, intensity, sexual desire, and or anxiety, in which there is an extreme absorption in another."[3] It is a feeling that is not reciprocated and is a one-way flow only. Often associated with youth, infatuation is can be referred to as "puppy love" suggesting the quality of intense affection without knowledge or judgment and seems to arise out of personal need in the presence of an attractive other. You meet someone. He's handsome. He may smile at you or say something kind, and you're hooked, you're infatuated. It's the stuff of our schoolgirl crushes, and sometimes it can develop further, but most often it doesn't. We would be wise to just let it end there.

Infatuation, unlike the other two phases of love, may be directed toward just about anyone and does not necessarily require personal contact, such as with a character in a novel, a movie star, a world-class athlete, or anyone else who is unavailable. I remember the last concert I attended; the crowd went crazy when the star stepped out on stage. This is not a new phenomenon. They say that famed Hungarian pianist Franz Liszt (1811-1886) was the object of affection from audiences that parallel those experienced by the young Frank Sinatra, Elvis Presley, and the Beatles.

The danger during the infatuation phase is that it clouds our judgment. The work place liaison, for example, in which one or two weeks of interaction builds infatuation to an intense level, can continue several months at a fever pitch, totally disrupting your emotional balance. During this phase you're so eager and sensitive to *any* signal from your object of infatuation that you often misinterpret the intent of any communication. You may even falsely assign "interest" to straightforward business e-mails. Now, how do you know if the signals you received were just hypersensitivity on your part or actually indicate interest on his part? The problem with understanding all of this is that none of it is black and white. Courtship comes in many forms, and that business e-mail may or may not be an overture of interest. It is hard to tell when your object of infatuation actually returns your interest.

Are you confused yet? You should be, because the infatuation stage of relationships is almost always frustrating. And there's no clear recommendation to be made at this stage. What we can say with certainty is that infatuation is one of the most blinding of emotions, and, in the absence of friendship and commitment, it eventually causes far more torment than pleasure. The best that can be said about it is that it doesn't last for long. If there is no meaningful contact with the object of our arousal, if the infatuation is not reciprocated, the feelings fade in time with consequences no more severe than the loss of time and energy devoted to our passion. It's either going to die a natural death, or it moves into reciprocal interest which then moves us from infatuation to the in-love state.

℞ THE IN-LOVE CONDITION

I can remember the swift stab of excitement that occurred when I first hoped that Darren was also interested in me. Because we met on the Internet, we knew we faced the challenge of overcoming geographic distance, but that didn't lessen the rush I felt when I received this e-mail, Darren's first words that launched us into romance:

```
Dear Elizabeth,

My mind responds to our first date in both
emotional and practical ways. The warmth and
commonality and richness and pleasure were
intense…we have established that we speak each
other's language, share each other's passion,
dream many of the same dreams, and enjoy enough
differences to make it interesting.
```

This, my friends, is classic of the next type or phase of love. As I read the e-mail I moved from infatuation to reciprocal interest, which is the in-love condition. It is really nothing more than a state of mutual infatuation. The reason I stated earlier in this chapter that "in love" was a troublemaker is because we think this phase is what we all want, that being in love is the goal. This is the romance, that out-of-breath feeling that we've been conditioned, by Hollywood and by our own dating, to interpret as the height of love. What I want you to realize is that the in-love condition is the passion that typically occurs early in the relationship. When we are in love we have hundreds if not thousands of different ways to accompany the overwhelming desire to express what we're feeling. It is sweet, it is wonderful, and, yes, it is the quality that drives the success of most films and romance novels. This is also where we encounter our culture's intense fascination with the idea of love-at-first-sight and the marriages that result from that instant romance.

The reality, however, is that research uncovers a different story. Only about 5 percent of marriages based on instant romance, marrying with thirty days of first meeting, actually survive.[4] Being in love is so intensely emotional that it often blots out important realities. We acknowledge the intense pleasure of being in love; however, just like infatuation leaves you irrational, so does this phase. One of my clients related the perfect story about this whole scenario. She said:

> I remember one of my dating relationships. It was with a man who had just separated from his wife, but I ignored that red flag and dealt only on the good things. There was so much emotion. We had our favorite restaurant, our favorite song to make love to. The notes, the flowers, all the acts that say "love" were everywhere. He even professed his love for me. I remember one evening as I was leaving his house, I looked at him waving to me from the window and thinking "I'm desperately in love with this man." "Desperately" should have been my warning, but I didn't pay any attention. I couldn't see the truth of the situation through all my emotion and I got deeper and deeper into a relationship that couldn't work. As it turned out, his goals and purposes were very different from mine—not to mention the fact that it was a classic rebound situation. As soon as his divorce proceedings started, I got dumped, and while I have suffered many broken hearts over the years, this one was the hardest.

The problem my client encountered is typical. Most people incorrectly think that arriving at or experiencing the in-love state is the pinnacle of their relationship. Researchers have also discovered that on average, the in-love condition lasts about two years. Say you get married at the one-and-a-half-year point; what are you going to do when the two years has run its course and you got another fifty-nine years or so to go? In fact, perhaps it's at this point, where the intense emotions decline, that people interpret the loss of emotion as an actual disappearance of love. They think because they don't feel intensely, that something is actually wrong with the relationship. Why don't you look back at your past relationships? More than likely, you'll remember when the in-love state had run its course in a long-term relationship. Think about what happened at that point. Did one of you break it off? Was there an affair? Did you feel abandoned within your relationship? Were you lonely? These are typical outcomes due to the likelihood that when the in-love state wanes, we miss its intensity and one or both people react with relationship-damaging behaviors.

But, I have great news. The gift of the next section is introducing you to an understanding that the in-love state can blossom into something far greater—the state of real love.

℞ REAL LOVE

So, real love is the good stuff, the mature love. Real love operates in a different context than the other two. It may have all the intensity of emotion, all the pleasure of the in-love condition, but it lives on a foundation of commitment and friendship. (Remember the points we covered in chapter 2 on "What Does 'Happily Ever After' Really Look Like?"; the three components of an exceptional marriage include the friendship dynamic, the love dynamic, and the foundation.) But, here's a hard pill to swallow. Your relationship will be challenged or even fail if you don't know about the transition from in love to real love. It is important to understand the *cause* of the deterioration of intense emotions of the in-love state as well as to prepare yourself for real love.

However, once you have prepared yourself for the transition and start to actively work toward real love, you will find that there is a warmer response to your beloved in which feelings of harmony, contentment, and cooperative accomplishment predominate. While the ecstasy of passion, the intense sweetness of the in-love state will happen from time to time throughout the duration of your relationship, the warmth and pleasure of companionship that comes with real love will be there for hundreds even thousands of hours every year. Mature love provides the adventure of discovering each other throughout your lifetime. Mature love provides the enjoyment of shared pursuits and the gift of laughter. And the most significant difference between mature love and the first two is that mature love does not have a time frame. It can last forever in the lives of those who experience it.

But instead of me continuing to tell you what the differences are, I'm going to defer to the distinctions that the experts have made between being in love and experiencing real love. And please don't fall into the trap of thinking that the researchers make it all too clinical, that they destroy the beauty and spontaneity of love. Think of it in this way: George Gershwin was ultimately knowledgeable of the structure and dynamics of music. Do you think this in any way diminished his enjoyment of playing for hours at just about any party he attended? Carl Lewis's Olympic championships were preceded by thousands of hours of exhausting training. Did the hard work diminish his pleasure? I would guess, no. Furthermore, the research can be very enlightening and can even enhance the pleasure in a relationship when you have a clearer understanding of where you're going. In fact, by looking at and applying what some of the best research says, you increase your chances of experiencing love at a richer, deeper, and more exciting level.

IN LOVE VERSUS REAL LOVE

To help you readjust your expectations and your thinking about love, the following table presents you with a side-by-side comparison between the in-love condition and real love. To make this comparison, I draw heavily from the work of Gary Chapman (*The Five Love Languages*)[5] and Erich Fromm (*The Art of Loving*).[6] Because of its importance, read through each group thoroughly and don't skim. (Married folks have also told me that this table is very helpful to them! So keep it around, as it might come in handy down the road one day.) To make your reading easier, I have grouped the points into four categories: duration, words, consequences, and a catch-all other. Enjoy!

Duration

In-Love Experience	Real Love
Researchers find that on average the in-love experience lasts about two years.	Many marriages never discover real love. For those who do, it can last a lifetime growing in richness for the duration.

The Words of the In-Love Person versus the Words of Those Experiencing Real Love

Illusions of the In-Love Experience	The Greater Reality of Real Love
1. My beloved is perfect (or the faults are cute or unimportant).	My beloved has challenges, flaws, and difficulties just as I have challenges, flaws, and difficulties.
2. Suggestions of others carry no weight. (How could feelings this strong be wrong?)	I am open to suggestions of others to alert us to things we may be blind to; in fact I seek out additional input from friends, counselors, books, tapes, videos, or other sources.
	Chart continued on next page...

...Chart continued from previous page	
Illusions of the In-Love Experience	**The Greater Reality of Real Love**
3. This feeling will last for ever.	Such intense feelings will happen from time to time in a good relationship.
4. This love will overcome all differences.	Differences need to be addressed thoughtfully and systematically to enhance the quality of our relationship or to determine whether the relationship should continue.
5. Nothing can ever come between us.	Many things may come between us, and it is well to safeguard the relationship by considering possible challenges.
6. Sex provides only the illusion of intimacy (remember that sexual arousal is unrelated to compatibility).	We continue to grow in real intimacy at all levels both physical and emotional.
7. Our love conquers all problems.	Thoughtful personal analysis, solid conflict-resolution skills, and occasional input from experts contribute to resolving our problems.
8. I could not possibly inflict discomfort or pain on my beloved.	There are times when I don't particularly like my partner and feel that a good kick in the seat of the pants might be therapeutic. I probably deserve a kick just as frequently.

Negative and Positive Consequences of the In-Love Experience and Real Love

In-Love Experience	Real Love
1. Loss of focus and concentration.	Focus returns. It is possible to think of other things.
2. Work and studies suffer.	Work and studies are enhanced by an excellent relationship.
3. Important issues are ignored.	Important issues are placed in their proper perspective.
	Chart continued on next page...

...Chart continued from previous page	
4. Important issues are ignored.	Important issues are placed in their proper perspective.
5. Disengages our reasoning abilities.	Reasoning abilities are free to be healthy and sound.
6. A deceiver that causes us to become deeply enmeshed in a relationship that cannot work.	We were not blinded by the romance. We chose each other knowing our strengths, our weaknesses and our love for each other.

Other Comparisons

In-Love Experience	Real Love
The in-love experience tends to just happen. We cannot choose to have it, and often it occurs at awkward times and is directed toward unlikely (often unacceptable) persons. It is rarely subject to conscious choice.	To love a partner is based on conscious choices and decisions to love. We express that love even when we don't feel like it and work progressively to nurture the growth of love.
The in-love experience renders all tasks effortless, requiring little discipline or conscious effort, and pushes us to do outlandish and unnatural things for each other.	Nurturance and continuation of the relationship requires disciplined, conscious effort to encourage each other to grow in important areas within the context of the relationship. It provides frequent reminders to the beloved that he or she is cherished and valued.
Has little interest in self-growth or nurturance of growth in the other. The focus is on having found rather than having become.	There is an appropriate focus on self growth and growth of my partner.

℞ HOW TO TRANSITION FROM IN LOVE TO REAL LOVE

As you transition from in love to real love, I want to share several insights with you. It takes work, commitment, and even fortitude to see it through. And if some of you are groaning, consider this: I was talking to a client one day about transitioning from being in love to realizing mature love and he gave the following response: "But this is too much work. Love should just happen." Unfortunately, he was experiencing the backlash of that mindset as he was ending yet another relationship following a horrific divorce, but his response was telling. We don't like to "work" at things that we think ought to be pleasurable. We are continuously coached by our culture that we should seek things that make our lives easier, and love is no different. Falling in love and then being in love is effortless, and we think that it should stay that way. But the transition from in love to real love is like someone growing up who moves from a lack of awareness of responsibility in childhood to embracing responsibility in adulthood. With infatuation and the in-love condition, there's no awareness of effort or responsibility. Our feelings create and drive the energy but are notoriously fickle and unreliable. Real love is embracing the responsibility of making choices that foster the different ideal components (as we outlined previously in chapter 2) of the relationship. The love we really should seek arises out of the health of these components instead of out of the energy of emotions.

As you start thinking about the transition from being in love to developing real love, remember that there are several things that work against us. As illustrated in the previous paragraph, we don't like to blend the idea of love and effort. Next, we don't want to leave behind the intense emotional high because, as I've noted before, we're culturally conditioned to believe that's the be-all and end-all of love. Finally, we don't like to treat love as something that we should think about logically. In spite of these barriers, my primary experience as a counselor overwhelming suggests that real love is worth the effort even though many never reach it and suffer greatly.

So, the remainder of this chapter is going to focus on a different stage of your relationship than that of any other portion of the book. While most of this book is dedicated to getting you ready to be romantically involved with someone, I'm going to indulge here in talking about what you do after you've been involved with someone for longer than two years, the make/break point in so many relationships. Since you now know that the stage of real love doesn't automatically happen, preparation and planning should begin between you and your partner long before the in-love experience wanes. While the primary focus of this book is on helping you find the right mate, my reason for talking about this important transition is so that when you do start dating, you can begin putting these pointers into place as a rich element of your dating experience. It will not only help show you if the man you are in love with is willing to "work" on the elements of a good marriage, but it will also enhance the relationship as it progresses. The two types of pointers that top my list as most useful and easily understood are to engage in romantic acts throughout your relationship and to understand each others' love languages.

Romantic Acts   ℞

Now here's the good news. The transition from being in love to real love is based simply on the concept of choosing to engage in what we call "romantic acts." These are acts that are designed to help our partner feel loved. These happen frequently, obsessively, even recklessly while in love; but when the glow fades, real love is kept vibrant by choosing to continue to do the acts that nurture the relationship. This has sound psychological grounding. Emotion is a response to actions. If we don't feel in love with our partner (a frequent occurrence in even the best relationships) doing the acts that express love rekindle the emotion.

I use the word *rekindle* on purpose here. We've all heard love being compared to a fire. Most often it's in the context of passion, but saying love is like a fire is actually very helpful in our quest to get from being in love to experiencing real love. First, the kind of fire that love is often equated with is actually the roaring yellow flames that look good but actually aren't as hot as the other parts of the fire. These types of fires also take huge amounts of fuel and will consume anything close, and while they look exciting, they won't necessarily last. The real heat of a fire comes from the blue flames and the red-hot coals that lie at the foundation of a fire. That level of heat depends on the type of fuel and how long the fire has been burning. Now, let's look at this analogy in terms of love. You're in love; the fire is roaring. It starts to die down, so you could pour on some lighter fluid, like the hot sex and giddiness, and blow the flames high. However, since the real heart of a fire is in its coals, in marriage, we're not necessarily after the yellow flames; we're after the really rich coals that are hot underneath the flames. My father was a master at building fires, and he taught me that when we use long-burning fuel and construct the fire with care and knowledge, we get those vibrant coals at the base that look like a living pulse. To get those fire-sustaining coals in a relationship takes a certain kind of fuel, the kind I'm presenting to you here. And just like my father's fires, a good bed of coals will sustain a lot—even a rainstorm now and then.

Love Languages   ℞

So, which acts keep the hot coals of love burning? I have a little book published by a division of Zondervan called *1001 Ways to Say I Love You*.[7]

The book goes on to list (as the title suggests) 1001 different things a man might do to help his wife feel loved. Flip the book over and it lists 1001 different things a woman might do to help her husband feel loved. I read through my half of the book and put checks next to items that might please my husband. However, while I had plenty of tick marks when I finished, I found that most of the suggested items weren't relevant and simply didn't fit Darren and his personality. Which poses the question: if I want love to develop and continue, which things should I do to help my partner feel loved? If I buy him gifts but he wishes for quality time together, I have missed the point. If you cook him a special meal but what he really wanted was for you to appreciate that he fixed the toilet, again, the point has been missed. How can we know which things to do to help our partner feel loved? (Remember, I'm writing this from the perspective that you've already found your mate). It is not a trivial question because mismatches of acts of appreciation and love happen millions of times every day. Two answers, taken from my own experience, come to mind:

First, ask your partner which things bring him pleasure. Similarly, during the process of getting to know your partner really well, the things that he appreciates will often emerge. But, do not make the mistake of assuming that a particular act brings pleasure, even if it is something you regularly do for him. Because we want to accept the overtures and gifts of our partners, we often will hesitate about letting them know we would prefer something else rather than hurt their feelings. Also be careful about merely copying what your friends do, those acts may or may not bring pleasure to your beloved. The idea then is to avoid like the plague the assumption that you "just know." Ask him, and find out, so that your acts of romance may be truly appreciated.

 The second action you might undertake is to read Gary Chapman's book *The Five Love Languages*, one of the most useful relationship books in print. In it he suggests that we speak different languages when expressing love to one another. The basis of the book's idea is that there is a great deal of marital discord because we attempt to express love to our partner but find ourselves speaking a different language than what our spouse understands.[8] In this context, great effort to express love may not be received or appreciated by the recipient of those efforts. I will list and briefly describe the five languages here, but treat yourself to the much more in depth picture that Chapman paints. Remember, if you put these principals into place in your dating relationship, you'll be ready and much more able to use them when you're married.

Here they are:

- **Words of Affirmation**: For many, words of encouragement, expressions of gratitude, heartfelt complements go a long way toward helping one's partner feel loved. As you come to know your partner better, it will become increasingly evident which words pack the highest voltage. For one, complementing how your partner looks may carry great weight, for another expressing appreciation for their actions ("Thanks for taking out the garbage!"), encouragement for their projects ("I know your presentation will be terrific!"), or uttering words of kindness ("I love the way you care for the children") may touch them more deeply.

- **Quality Time**: How many stories are told of one partner spending so much time pursuing his or her career that little time is spent together and the relationship withers and often dies. All the gifts or verbal compliments in the world cannot make up for the absence of the relationship that is the consequence of such neglect. If you both operate on a tight timetable, then schedule times to be together and make sure those times are systematically honored. Further, realize that spending time together may require more than passive involvement such as watching TV or a movie. While some passive time together may be important, quality conversations or romantic getaways are almost always an important component of quality time.

- **Receiving Gifts**: Chapman points out that practically all cultures use gift-giving as an important way of expressing love. Gifts are often actual objects that one can look at years later and remember not so much the gift as the love that inspired the gift. However, gifts that express love, but do not last, may be equally important. We know this as women because we like to receive (as well as give) flowers. But, don't think for a minute that your special guy wouldn't like to get flowers too sometimes. I remember one year when I surprised Darren on his birthday by walking into his university lecture with a long stemmed red rose and a big block of his favorite cheese. He's talked about it ever since. Whatever you choose to give, make sure that it speaks his language, not yours. And, also make sure that you're not giving presents in lieu of something else. One tragedy of gift giving is when our beloved is hungry for something else—physical touch or words of affirmation, for instance—and we've given an expensive gift as a substitute or out of guilt for not providing emotional needs.

- **Acts of Service**: Clean the house, cook the meals, take out the garbage, wash the car, fix the toilet, change the diapers, help with an assignment—the list is endless. For those who value this language, such acts may be a powerful expression of love. The practical behaviors that make another's life easier are often part and parcel of the dynamics of a loving relationship. As with gifts, do be careful that the acts are done from the heart. If you do them because you fear the consequences of not doing them, then it becomes something other than the expression of a love language.

- **Physical Touch**: It is the rare individual for whom physical touch is not important to the nurturing of an excellent relationship. Touch can, of course, cover the entire spectrum from linking little fingers to sexual intimacy. There is huge variation from person to person on which type of touch communicates most effectively. For one it may be frequent embraces, rubbing shoulders or running fingers through hair, playing footsie under the table, nesting in front of a cozy fire, or a wide array of sexual activities. Perhaps more so than in other area it is important to determine which type of touch brings your partner greatest pleasure; once you know what that is, then provide it in abundance.

It's not really hard to move from in-love condition to real love once you understand the dynamics, and my husband and I have found wonderful moments of humor and poignancy as we've transitioned from one to the other. This work doesn't have to be laborious. While the remainder of the book is devoted to helping find a man that is compatible with you, keep in mind that even as compatibility provides the foundation for a many-splendored marriage, love, real love, is a massive cornerstone. Without it, no marriage exists in all the richness that it was designed to have. Remember that love cannot overcome the barriers of incompatibility, but when you have done your homework and have found your ideal man, you will be ready to create a love with your partner that lasts a lifetime.

STEP ONE OF THE PRE*fix* PROCESS

Take a Look Inward

WHERE ARE YOU NOW?

Congratulations! You have completed your prerequisites. You know what has misled your thinking before, and have unraveled some of the mysteries of love. You are armed with knowledge of what goes into having a successful marriage, but you still have the somewhat daunting task of finding your Mr. Right. While that task may seem overwhelming, it is very possible, even pleasurable, to do so.

In a counseling session one day, I was faced with a single mother named Ruth who had been through a difficult divorce. She sat looking down into her lap, her face a picture of defeat. Quietly she asked, "How will I ever know if I'm ready to date again? When I said my marriage vows, I meant them. I loved my husband and I believed that we would have a good marriage. Now I don't trust myself, and I have my two children to think about." This took me back to my years as a single parent of twin daughters. I remember the burden of loving, raising, and providing for them. It was difficult to find time for myself, much less to contemplate dating again. One of my biggest questions was, "How do I date in a way that doesn't involve the children before I know the relationship has a chance." Then there was the emotional turmoil and energy that dating brings on.

What I didn't know then was that I was not asking the right questions, that I didn't even have the right starting point. Hundreds of books address how to find a lover, how to make anyone fall in love with you, how to cultivate a successful marriage, how to cope with a disastrous one, or if unsuccessful, how to divorce.

What was missing was a straightforward guide to finding a compatible partner based on the factual and the emotional factors that contribute to marital success. That's what the next element of the compatibility code is all about: the pre*fix* process, asking the right questions so you can make the right decisions.

But what does that look like in real life? You're in your thirties, forties, even fifties or sixties. You've been burned in love, maybe a lot, maybe a little. You might be divorced, or you have looked and looked for Mr. Right, but every time you come close—or not so close—he turns out to be just another example of someone who you thought was "the one." A friend of mine once told me about a cartoon that she had plastered on her refrigerator. It had a girl hugging a monster and the caption read "but he has so much potential." She couldn't remember the cartoonist's name, but she told me that she called all her Mr. Wrong's "potential monsters." I found it a fitting title and it pointed to the real life story that happens over and over.

We all know it well. You meet someone, and hope reignites the dream that he's going to sweep you off your feet and you'll live "happily ever after." He seems to have everything you ever wanted. But, days, months, even years into the relationship, you find that the promise of the fairy-tale ending isn't happening for you. Your Mr. Right has turned into the "potential monster," so much promise, but so little actual compatibility. Because this has happened to you too many times, you are now gun shy. You're definitely suspicious of the fairy-tale ending. Maybe you're too tired to start dating or too busy to waste time dating the wrong person. But as I said, I've been there too.

Fulfilling and magnificent marriages can happen. You can beat the ridiculously high odds that your marriage will end in divorce. But I'll give you a warning as we start step one of the pre*fix* process. It contains a lot more realism and far fewer "stars in your eyes," than you may be accustomed to. You are going to be required to first take a hard look at yourself and discover if you have any residual anger, devastation, or jealousy. These are emotional germs, potentially lethal to any form of human association, and if they linger on from one liaison to another, they will infect every one of your subsequent relationships. Once you have declared yourself emotionally healthy enough to proceed, you are going to be asked to find out about yourself, your personality traits first and then those qualities that make up the fundamental you. I call these last traits your essence qualities because they are those things that, if you changed them, then you would no longer be you. You need to have a good idea of what your essences are because they help you figure out what kind of person is most compatible with you.

Marriage is a partnership, and while it may sound unromantic, if you approach the process a little more like a business, you will go about finding your life mate armed with a clear picture of what "perfect" means for you. I want to equip you with a better understanding of your starting point and to help you improve your confidence in your ability to enter into a fulfilling marriage relationship that will last a lifetime.

Chapter 4

YIKES! AM I READY?

*Handling the Emotional Germs
from Previous Relationships*

re you familiar with the warning that accompanies most
exercise programs, the one that says: "consult a doctor before
you start this or any other form of strenuous activity?" It's
there for a reason. The physical health of a person depends on
the strength of his or her systems, from the skeletal and cardiovascular
to the all important immune system. Similarly, your "relational" health
is dependent on maintaining balance in the psychological systems,
and, before you begin a program of dating, it's important to assess how
healthy you are emotionally. Now that you understand that the fairy-
tale model leaves you cold after sunset, and we have an image of the
ideal components of a great marriage, it's time for you to get a check-up
on your emotional health before you begin a serious search for your real
"Mr. Right."

Emotions are a lot like bacteria, which are actually peculiar little entities. Some strains, the pathogenic ones we call germs, can make you very ill, but other strains are absolutely vital to our health. Emotions, especially strong ones, work much like bacteria. Strong emotions that are out of control, particularly those left over from a broken relationship—the bad bacteria, as it were—can cause havoc in a new relationship.

The point that I'm getting at here is that in order to start a new healthy relationship, it's important to be in relatively decent emotional health. I say relative because you don't have to be in perfect shape to start the process of looking for a mate and then beginning a relationship. No-one is ever perfect. Looking at it through the lens of the germ analogy, we're never without some level of exposure to germs. Our ability to fight off the attack of germs depends on how healthy—or not—we are. My hope is that by the end of the chapter, you'll have a better idea of where you are on the emotional health continuum and know what you need to do to heal from the negative effects of accumulated strong emotions.

WARNING: STRONG EMOTIONS CLOUD JUDGMENT

℞ There's no nice way to put this: research documents that *when you are feeling intense emotions, you should not make any kind of relationship decisions, period.* In fact, and I can't stress this strongly enough, you should avoid all major decisions in the face of strong emotions. While there are many intense feelings that can affect your relational health, in this chapter, we will focus on only those emotions that have accumulated from the ravages of broken relationships.

Before you move forward in deciding whether you are ready to date again, you must not only be willing to assess your emotional health, but also be able to determine if you are experiencing emotional and psychological damage from past relationships. Recognition is always the first step of recovery, and you may need to face up to some hard truths about the strong emotions that follow a break up. It's likely that you have experienced one or more of these: the sexual desire gone out of control because you crave closeness, the jealousy, outrage, even hatred, that can come from a broken heart. Other emotions may stem from the awful cycle of break-up, reunite, break-up, reunite that traps your self-esteem and leaves you in depression or out of control.

Just to give you another viewpoint on this: look at how you feel once a month. I made it a rule a long time ago not to schedule important meetings when I'm suppose to start my period because I'm so impatient and my perspective seems to be skewed. Now, think about this. All of these emotions are in me the other twenty-six or so days of the month, but because of the heightened hormonal stress of a period, they flare up. Likewise, when our immune system is lowered because of stress, lack of sleep, or poor nutrition, we become more susceptible to the germs that are constantly flying around. The germs are always there; whether or not we succumb to the infection depends on our health. The same holds true for our emotions.

Because a healthy emotional state is vital to the success of a relationship, it is important that you find out at what point the emotions render you dysfunctional. In other words, I want to help you determine whether you are experiencing a normal flare-up of emotions or whether those emotions are consistently controlling you.

The purpose of this chapter is to give you guidance on whether you are ready to date again. So I use anger, devastation, pain, need, and jealousy as prominent examples of the types of emotional germs you should look for and how to respond to their presence. However, I want to make sure you are aware that there are many other types of damaging issues you may be dealing with from a broken relationship such as feelings of guilt, cynicism, powerlessness, rejection, abandonment and violation. I caution you again, if you are experiencing consistent or insidious control by any one of these "germs," or any other damaging emotions, then you should not move forward with the work I ask you to do in this book—until, that is, you have addressed them. Inadequate resolution will negatively affect your ability to do the next steps of this process of pre*fix*ing your marriage.

In the event, after reviewing this chapter, you feel you have reasonable emotional health and are ready to move forward, keep in mind that you still should still be aware of the clouding nature of strong emotions. Think about it. Even intense excitement can create "gullible errors." You fall "in love" with some gadget or gizmo or gorgeous pair of shoes. You *just have* to buy it, but then you end up with a closet or a garage filled with worthless stuff that you've no idea what to do with. Recognizing and warding against the influence of these types of emotions and biases while you date is of such great importance that we devote more time to it in chapter 9 as we take a look outward.

Now we are going to look at each of our prominent germs individually and offer ways to go about handling them.

℞ *Anger*

I start with anger because it is one of the most striking reactions to a broken relationship. In our germ analogy, it is like the knife that inflicts the damage, which opens the wounds that can then get infected with devastation or jealousy. Most of the people that I counsel, before, during, or after their separation or divorce, experience some level of anger, which is normal. However, it is vital to address it early because if you don't, it can harm you for a long time, especially if you either knowingly or unknowingly choose to nurse it.

Sometimes, anger is stimulated in you by immediate and observable causes such as betrayal, infidelity, just plain meanness, or at worst, violation. Other times there has been no overt effort to hurt one another; it's just that the relationship didn't work out. Even then, anger is often the result.

Much of the reason for angry, aggressive feelings is due simply to what psychologists call "pain-elicited aggression." [1] It applies to animals; it applies to humans. It works this way. In an experiment, two sets of laboratory animals are placed in a cage with many other animals. In one instance there is a loud piercing noise; in the other there is none. The noise is external; it is not caused by any of the animals, but researchers observe far greater levels of aggressive behavior among the animals in the distressing situation than among animals in the control group with no noise. Similar experiments have involved humans with similar results.

My husband, prior to meeting me, actually experienced this type of reaction when he finally broke off an "on-again-off-again" five-year romantic relationship. He was emotionally devastated for several months, as I imagine her to have been as well. But in addition to the devastation, Darren also experienced the effect of heightened anger. He had extreme negative thoughts towards his ex-girlfriend. He didn't want her to be successful in business, in relationships, or in any other area of her life. However, because he knew about pain-elicited aggression, he realized, even in his worst moments, that he didn't really wish her ill. He was just hurting and the aggressive thoughts were a consequence of the pain he was feeling. Because he knew the cause of his feelings, the knowledge allowed insight and clarity into his own thought processes. He later shared with me that about two months after the break-up, while he was still deeply feeling the loss of the relationship, an acquaintance came up to him with bright eager eyes, and without realizing his single status said, "Oh Darren, I hear that the two of you are engaged!" He said, "We were, but I broke up with her two months ago!" Her response astonished him: "Oh you must feel really guilty!" He responded, "Not at all; we tried really hard for five years, and it simply didn't work out. I still wish her well even though I recognize we weren't right for each other." Because of his knowledge of the anger that can follow emotional pain, he exhibited a level of insight and calmness even while in pain. Several years later there is, of course, not a shred of negative feeling toward the woman.

C.S. Lewis, author of the favorite children's series, *The Chronicles of Narnia*, gives us another way to look at anger. In the story of his spiritual odyssey, *Surprised by Joy*, he speaks of his entry into the British Army in 1917 during World War I. He says, "It was, of course, awful; but the 'of course' blunted the pain. I never thought it would be wonderful." [2] One could speak of a break-up in the same way: "It was, of course, awful," but by acknowledging the "of course," you can blunt the pain. After a break-up, when you know you're going to be in pain, you can also recognize that you may have destructive thoughts towards that person. But you can gain assurance by recognizing that the anger and the potentially destructive thoughts that come with it do not carry real substance.

The problem, of course, happens when the anger isn't resolved. There is actually a five-step process that a person can go through to effectively deal with their anger. The five steps are listed below with clarification following each one:

1. **Admit** it: There are some who don't like to admit they are angry. However, to begin resolution you need to be objectively aware of just how angry, outraged, incensed, furious, or irate you really are. When you acknowledge the severity of your emotions, then you can begin to do something about them.

2. **Vent** it: There are two types of venting: physical release, and cognitive/emotional release. Physical release (beat a punching bag, run twenty miles, scream at the top of your lungs) may assist in immediate reduction of emotions, but its benefit is only temporary. The cognitive and emotional form of venting is required. This type of venting is typically in the form of talking through your feelings with an objective other person. This allows you to externalize those feelings, and causes them to lose power. The person you speak with could be a therapist or counselor, or it could be several of your friends. Just don't jeopardize a friendship by dumping too much negative emotion on one person.

3. **Plan** it: Once emotion has reduced to the point that you are thinking more rationally (this might take months if the emotions are extreme) then you begin to plan how to deal with feelings or to deal with the circumstances that have caused them. This is where a professional counselor can prove to be invaluable. They have access to a wide array of resources to assist you in dealing with anger. The planning may focus on control of your own emotions; pursuing healthy alternative activities; understanding the dynamics of what has happened; and other times eradicating irrational thought patterns.

4. **Do** it: Once planned, the next step is to discipline yourself to carry out the activities. Good intentions don't work here; do what's on the list. One interesting example (assuming that this has been planned) is to write a barnburner of a letter expressing your outrage at the jerk who inflicted this pain on you. Don't hold back, this letter should skin the hide off of a billy goat! Then read it carefully to make sure you have included everything—add missing details. Read it again, several times if you like…and burn the letter. You have gotten it out. When externalized, emotions lose their power. There are hundreds more techniques that a therapist would help you fit to your situation, but it's up to you to carry them out.

5. **Forget** it: Some find this a strange final step. The reality is that if you have completed the four steps listed above, forgetting will happen as a natural consequence. As you pursue other meaningful activities, the powerful emotions will eventually die a natural death. In some exceptionally difficult cases more effort is required and there are therapists who devote their entire practice to helping people forget painful events.

Do you want to know what doesn't work? Just skip the first four steps and try to perform step number five. The effort to forget painful emotions without thorough processing of steps one to four is what psychologists call repression. You internalize all the poison and find that its ravaging effects will continue to haunt you for a very long time, sometimes for a lifetime.

At the end of this process, you won't have forgotten the events that occurred, but the emotional horror and the anger that results from it can be entirely erased. Once you have *resolved* the issue by going through the steps of externalization (steps one and two) and taking the appropriate action (steps three, four, and five), then you can move on with your life. As suggested above, unresolved, it has the potential to turn into a cancer that eats away at your emotional health.

Devastation R_X

If anger is the initial knife wound to your heart, then devastation is the acute infection that can follow a break-up. While acute infections are sometimes overwhelmingly painful and can leave you incapacitated for a while, with immediate and appropriate care, they can heal.

We all know that breaking up with someone you've been in love with is likely to be devastating, that awful feeling of being overwhelmed by shock or grief because your world has been turned upside down. Like anger, it is a natural emotion resulting from the loss of a relationship. But what are the right treatments? How do you recover from the devastation? A frequent, but disastrous response is to rush into a new relationship. Most of us have either experienced or seen friends go through the heartache of a romance initiated too soon, the classic "rebound."

Devastation is so multi-faceted and completely overwhelming that you need to equip yourself with the techniques to deal with it, and then do the work of handling the feelings. Just like with the loss of a loved one, there is a required grieving period. While it is not possible to shorten the length of time associated with healing, it is very possible, using appropriate methods, to ensure that recovering from devastation does not extend beyond what is necessary. On the other hand, using poor choices, it is quite possible to extend the feelings of devastation long beyond the needed healing period. Here's how: remember your lowest moment, the most terrifying fear, the most gut-wrenching agony, the most intense rage, how badly mistreated you were. Take your pick or try to remember all of them. Vividly relive them. Your reward will be to experience a feeling of misery just as severe as that felt immediately after the break. Whenever emotions begin to wane, repeat the process. This will allow you to remain devastated for your entire life and to spend your last moments remembering how awful it was.

If you would prefer to not follow that pattern, there are specific R_X
guidelines to speed recovery from devastation. Suggestions provided by
the experts include:

- **Closure**: First and foremost, come to an irrevocable decision that the relationship is over and you will not return to it. While you remain in ambiguity about whether you should or shouldn't, you will remain in turmoil. Only the closed and locked door allows the process of healing to begin. "But can't we be just friends?" I hear someone cry. The answer is a definitive no! Maybe a couple years later after full recovery, but don't even think about it now. Break off all contact.

- **Externalize**: Externalize the negative reactions, talk through your feelings, write them in diaries, accept that you are hurting, but don't cling to it. The methods of externalization are numerous: speak with a number of friends (but don't over-burden any one of them), go to groups that allow recovery such a Divorce Anonymous, or go see some type of qualified counselor or therapist. Whatever the cost, this phase must be done for emotionally healthy recovery to occur.

- **Appropriate process**: Once you have satisfactorily worked through the negativity, don't allow your mind to obsess on it. The five-step process I noted above for anger works just as well for handling devastation. Here it is again so you can specifically consider your feelings of devastation—if you have them. They are: 1) admit the pain, anger, etc.; 2) vent or externalize it; 3) determine a course of response; 4) do it by carrying out your plan; and 5) forget it. One needs to have completed the first four steps prior to forgetting. Once the steps are completed then a natural death of the damaging feelings can occur by shifting thoughts when "the topic" comes up.

- **Activities**: Engage in activities that you enjoy even though there is a sense of desperation that you are only doing this to forget some-thing painful. Accept that! Don't demand that the activities, early in the process, bring much pleasure. Usually they won't because you are still hurting too much. Do them anyway and the pain will eventually subside.

- **Maintain routine**: Don't stop living to sit and stew. I know one individual who would continue to prepare a real meal despite the fact that it was only for herself. If you are working, continue; if going to school, don't drop out; if you have a regular exercise program, keep it up. Once again, don't expect much joy out of these activities, just do them until, in the fullness of time, the joy begins to return. If your devastation is too great to maintain routine, consider the next item.

- **Find a safe place**: Sometimes it is good to get away from your current environment to a safe place, one that doesn't re-stimulate the memory of the devastation. For some, that may be moving back in with your parents for a while. Your safe place is entirely up to you, but physically removing yourself from the dangerous environment can help the healing process begin.

- **Avoid the torture chamber**: Avoid situations or settings that allow the pain to settle in. For example, don't go to bed early. Wait until you are so tired you will fall asleep easily. Avoid times or locations when the feelings of pain may be the greatest, such as Friday nights by yourself, or weekends bumping around the empty rooms in your home. Instead, get out and join an exercise, hobby, or community-service group, invite friends over, develop an after work get-together or movie night, anything that will get you away from places that invite painful reflection.

- **Rich network**: Maintain a rich network of friends. In a 1996 study that my husband conducted on factors that contribute to or detract from divorce recovery, he found that a rich network of friends and family was the greatest single predictor of emotional restoration. It will work just as well when recovering from any sort of relationship break.

- **Nurturing physical closeness**: Involve yourself in settings that allow for non-sexual physical contact. In the same study, the second greatest predictor of recovery was physical contact outside of a sexual setting. Enjoy affection from family and friends; get an affectionate, non-judgmental pet (avoid frogs, salamanders, and tarantulas); get a massage, a facial, a manicure, a haircut, but, at this phase, don't cross the line into sexuality.

- **Avoid sexual contact**: Avoid sexual or romantic entanglements during this phase. As mentioned above, while physical closeness was the second greatest predictor of recovery from divorce, sexual involvement was the second greatest detriment.

The feelings of devastation are hard to endure, but the speed with which they dissolve is dependent on how well you follow an appropriate healing process. If you find that you can't pull yourself out of the quagmire of devastation-caused emotions, seek qualified help. Like repressed anger, this too can metastasize if left unhandled.

R̥ *Pain and Need*

Pain and need are strong motivators in many scenarios, not just relationships, and so therefore these two emotions can be classed as an emotional germ left after the battle of divorce and separation. Unfortunately, the emotion of pain can also occur due to other horrific events, such as loss of a loved one or being fired from a job. Rejection and loss often prompt intense need and people are often drawn to others in similar states of pain and need. This response to pain and need also clouds judgment.

When my husband experienced divorce in 1990, to assist in recovery he attended group meetings with Divorce Anonymous. There he was in contact with one huge bundle of hurting people. As he observed behaviors and interactions over the months, he began to see the effect of need and pain. People would become involved with each other, in some cases marry, but the results were almost always disastrous. Research has revealed that both conditions (need and pain) have the power to increase the search for comfort in the presence of others, and to eliminate or severely compromise most forms of rational thought in choices made. People experiencing pain and need are often attracted to each other like magnets. I hurt, you hurt, and it feels so scrumptious to be held tightly in an intimate embrace. But then the couple awakes the next morning (or even much later) to find that no other similarities exist—other than shared pain and need. Guilt and embarrassment raise their ugly heads out of the bed of violation of important boundaries. Two people can have intense physical and emotional arousal in a relationship with the intensity masking total incompatibility. The human need for comfort in relationships is so powerful and self-evident that research only restates the obvious.[3]

In considering the need one has to be in a relationship when hurting, the composite psychologist would start off with the following cold statement: "Until the pain is diminished and the hunger to date or be in a relationship is reduced to the point that you are comfortable being single, it is better to avoid any relationship that extends beyond friendship." The statement may be absolutely correct and valid, but somehow it ignores the agonies people experience in their need for intimacy. I have experienced the trauma of divorce and the pain seethed inside of me until I became exhausted. I found that, consistent with sound counseling advice, I benefited from placing myself in a context that allowed me to be nurtured, to be cared for by warm, positive people.

In a recent study conducted by my husband and colleagues, they explored, with a sample of 229 divorced individuals, factors that enhanced or detracted from divorce recovery. And as mentioned in recovering from devastation, non-sexual physical closeness and a strong support network of friends are the top two predictors of recovery. By contrast, sexual involvement during the divorce process ranks as the second most destructive factor, closely following negative relationships with the former spouse. So, while I empathize with your pain and need, this study supports the cool statement of the professionals: "get over it before you start dating again."

Jealousy ℞

Jealousy comes in many forms, some of which are appropriate and some inappropriate. In the Bible, God is spoken of as "jealous of His own people." Appropriate jealousy is typically associated with a committed relationship in which those feelings surface when the quality or even the existence of that relationship is threatened. This is a good thing. It provides guidance for behavior. However, in the context that we're looking at, the jealousy that can arise at the end of a relationship can act like a puncture wound. It goes deep, and if it's not properly cared for, the surface of the wound can heal over but the infection is still there, festering.

First we need to identify what jealousy is. Webster's provides several definitions: "1) intolerant of rivalry or unfaithfulness; 2) disposed to suspect rivalry or unfaithfulness; 3) apprehensive of the loss of one another's exclusive devotion; 4) hostility toward a rival or one thought to have an advantage; 5) vigilant in guarding a possession; and 6) distrustfully watching." [4] This multi-faceted definition provides some insight into the issue of jealousy, but for sake of this discussion, we will limit ourselves in application.

Here, we are not examining the jealousy that exists within a marriage in which we think our relationship is being threatened. Nor are we considering the close equivalent, that is, jealousy over the threat to an ongoing committed dating relationship. Rather, we will focus on the feelings of jealousy following the end of a relationship, which, based on the definitions I just gave you, is usually a false jealousy. Let's apply the various definitions that reveal false jealousy, definitions one and two: "intolerant of rivalry or unfaithfulness" and "disposed to suspect rivalry or unfaithfulness." Because you're no longer in the relationship, the "other woman" is not your rival and no unfaithfulness can occur in a relationship that doesn't exist. Definition three: "apprehensive of the loss of one another's exclusive devotion." You've already lost it; apprehension has turned into reality. Now you need to deal with it. Definitions five and six: "vigilant in guarding a possession" and "distrustfully watching." No amount of vigilance is appropriate now; your ex is not your possession. And while you may feel an overwhelming, even instinctive urge to watch, the behavior is personally destructive.

If you deeply cared for and desired the person that is no longer yours, it is very natural to feel the emotions presented in definition four: "hostility toward a rival or one thought to have an advantage." This jealousy is not only real, but it is normal to feel badly toward someone who now has the advantage of sharing a relationship with the one you loved. It is painful, and it will take some time to get over it. Awareness and heartache from it is further augmented in the numerous movies (*My Best Friend's Wedding*; *When Harry Met Sally*) that portray the intensity of jealousy felt when someone they broke-up with, even years before, gets married. Let's bring it closer to home. We've probably all experienced breaking up with a long-term romantic partner and then, sometime later, seeing him with someone else. It is the rare individual (assuming she still has feelings for the other) who does not feel the stab of agony that leaves her dysfunctional for the next few hours, days, weeks, or even months when this happens. Elton John sings it straight as he watches two silhouettes in the window of his darling's house and knows that the relationship is over: "Not knowing where or when I'll see you … My friends all say don't go to pieces. I say that's, fine but if I lose, I want to know who's in my footsteps, I want to know who wears these shoes." [5]

℞ If you recognize that you're consistently grappling with feelings of jealousy, let's take a look at some appropriate steps to handle it, and help you move on:

- **Accept that the relationship is over**: When the relationship is over, it's over. The longer you live in ambiguity about whether a relationship is finished, the longer you condemn yourself to a flood of destabilizing emotions. As with a divorce, healing can begin only when the finality of that reality is fully accepted and internalized. With any type of ended relationship, the same principle applies. Those who are unable to accept this will live a life of tormented vacillation until a definitive choice is made.

- **Accept that most forms of jealousy are now inappropriate**: Most sensations of jealousy regarding someone with whom you no longer have a relationship are unhealthy. He is not attached to you. He is now available to others. He may date and be involved with whomever he wishes. This is no longer your concern. Yes, I know it hurts, but this is the type of jealousy that you need to train yourself away from, and to do that go back to the first point.

- **A change of setting may be desirable**: A sense of loss is normal; even an initial sense of insane jealousy towards one who now has the person you once loved is also very natural. This is a challenge so distressing to some that they move far away so they don't have to see it. This may be, in some instances, a wise choice. There is no advantage served by being constantly around the source of your pain. If you are suffering severely about watching the man you love fall in love with someone else, then thoughtfully consider getting away from it. Affirm along with Linus from the *Peanuts* cartoon—tongue in cheek of course: "There is no problem so big that it cannot be run away from." [6]

- **Try the rubber band**: During recovery, involve yourself in supportive friendships and refuse to allow your mind to dwell on your loss. A simple method sounds ridiculous but is rooted in rock solid psychological theory and is very effective. It is straight out of B.F. Skinner's principles of reinforcement. [7] Put a rubber band around your wrist. Whenever a thought of the other begins to emerge, snap the rubber band. If you try this when you're still in the "raw" phase of the breakup, you will only get sore wrists. But if recovery has begun, this method will help wipe out thoughts of the former partner much more quickly than any other process I know of.

- **Develop an alternative focus:** A common response to a break-up is to vigilantly watch your ex. Realize first that you are engaging in totally self-destructive behavior. And while the advice is simple—just stop!—the application may be difficult. One of the best ways to do this is to develop an alternative focus. Actually both responses are crucial: quit watching *and* develop an alternative focus. The idea here is to find a subject or interest that will occupy your mind and give it a focus that doesn't include the activities of people from your lost relationship. The challenge you will face is that the alternative may not fulfill the same need. For instance, while taking up racquetball is at least mentally and physically engaging it is not the same as lost intimacy. My husband applied the principle of alternative focus successfully during his divorce in 1990 while finishing his Ph.D. at UCLA. Like so many others, he was depressive, suicidal, in a state of emotional chaos, but he determined that this event would not defeat him and that he would complete the Ph.D. successfully. The energy generated from the trauma must have been great; he finished the degree in three years, four years faster than the average Psychology Ph.D. at that institution! As a further bonus, the trauma from the divorce was completely purged by the time he finished.

In contrast to the situation above, there is a kind of jealousy that leads to chronic poor emotional health, the kind that is neurotic, meaning that the feelings continue far beyond what is normal, useful, or functional. If, as you read this chapter, you realize that you are harboring too much jealousy, then it is time to consider allowing someone who is trained to help you deal with this emotion.

℞ An Example of When One Should Seek Professional Help

Okay, you say. I get that emotional germs, if not handled, can adversely affect me in my new relationship. But, how will I really know when I need to seek more help because I can't go it alone? To answer this, let's take a look at a hypothetical woman who tried to do it herself but didn't succeed, and then contrast it with her healing process with the aid of a professional. Let us first create some details: she had been through a divorce after a ten-year relationship that ended while her husband was having an affair. There was a nasty custody battle over the children. There has been financial devastation as a result of the divorce, not only from the crushing legal debt but also from loosing half the former family income. She may even have found that she temporarily had to rely on friends and family for finances or housing. There is continued friction over visitation and custody issues. An unusual story? No, it has distressingly been repeated a million times at all economic levels.

Her own efforts: She knows that her feelings continue to seethe and swirl. She's devastated and angry. She follows the steps I suggest above dealing with those emotions, but there are so many ongoing consequences to her relationship that she is unable to forget the violation and betrayal or the ongoing pain. She tries to think positive. She tries to get over it.

But every contact with her ex and his new girlfriend (or even new wife) reopens the wounds, and jealousy lurks beneath the surface. The children are suffering; her life spins out of control. Even after the custody issues have been smoothed out (this may take several years) and the daily events do not create the same level of devastation, the damage remains vivid and many things may cue the former devastation. She tries to not think so negatively about him, but has little success. She is quite able, with minimal effort, to recreate all the horror surrounding the original events. She seeks solace in a relationship, but the former issues have not been resolved and the romantic partner wisely recedes suggesting that perhaps this is a little too much reality of the past to endure at present. The negative emotions eventually brew into an underlying current of bitterness and hostility. She could go to her grave carrying this load and spend a lifetime, because of her volatility, hurting more people than she helps. But, before she dooms herself to that fate, she heeds my advice—as a last resort in her case—and seeks professional help.

Professional help: In a counseling session, the professional will initially show this woman empathy, and he or she will listen until the devastated woman feels that she has been heard. The therapist will then guide this woman through a process of healing acceptance and the "unconditional positive regard" made famous by Carl Rogers.[8] At the appropriate time, the professional will help place the entire mess in perspective. He or she will make clear a number of realities:

- She has been hurt badly.
- Two kinds of healing are required: a) a resolving of ongoing crises and b) a cognitive and emotional shift that allows her to respond more usefully to the present (or former) horror.
- There is a "grieving period" associated with any major loss. While it is not possible to shorten or speed up the process, by taking the right action it is possible for healing to be completed in the minimum amount of time.
- Complete healing does not mean that she forgets the events but that she can remember them without an emotional response. Since children are involved, there will be ongoing irritations and there may be new events that cue anger. Through therapy she will be taught to internalize a certain toughness and respond appropriately to ongoing challenges.

- Without professional guidance many convince themselves that they will be scarred for life. With professional help this woman can not only avoid being scarred but also actually be a better person for having gone through the valley of the shadow.

- The therapist will help her create a picture of what she eventually wants to be and arrive at—personally, financially, relationally. Then an outline will be determined, with step-by-step procedures for her to gradually move toward that reality.

- During the process the counselor will encourage and guide her through the many set backs she will certainly encounter.

Not all people mired in anger, devastation, jealousy, or other emotional issues resulting from broken relationships require professional help. Some are able to follow the pattern of responses I gave you in each section, and successfully negotiate a recovery that doesn't extend beyond the necessary "grieving period." But there are many who would benefit greatly from the assistance of a professional. If you're one of them, don't cheat yourself by trying to do it yourself.

R̶x **WHAT ARE YOU DOING TO BUILD YOUR EMOTIONAL IMMUNE SYSTEM?**

Most of this chapter has been devoted to helping you recognize unhealthy emotions and guide you through a process of handling them. However, know that the best measures, in health and in emotions, are preventative. I want to leave you with the idea that you can build up your emotional immune system so that when crisis hits, it doesn't make you sick and land you in the therapist's office. You can start by reading good books on how to achieve and maintain your emotional health. You can observe and talk to people who are in or have experienced healthy relationships. One of the best ways to find out how to make a million dollars is by talking to a millionaire or two, and it is no different in relationships. You can gain a wealth of information from these relationally seasoned and successful people.

However, there can be major sources of emotional germs right under your nose, and you would be wise to coat them with psychological Neosporin—or for you natural girls, tea tree oil—so that the infection can't take hold. A major source of emotional germs comes from the people who are chronically emotionally unhealthy themselves. It could be individuals, groups, or organizations who seem to function from a negative mindset, some of whom could be your regular association of friends. How many parties have you gone to where the guys are in the corner talking about guy things: race cars, hunting, sports, and the women are in the corner talking about their children, of course, but they're also talking about who's sleeping with whom and how dissatisfied they are? You simply don't want to systematically tax your emotional immune system with energy draining, depressing information.

Focus on the good emotions. Build them, the joy, the laughter, the sweet strong sense of deep friendship. Instead of dwelling on the negative, we need to seek company that encourages and affirms our goal of improving ourselves. These positive relationships are a component of becoming ready to embark on finding a life partner who is right for us. They assist in developing a lasting partnership that doesn't end in heartache, loss, loneliness, and pain but rather blossoms into a lasting strong marriage based on friendship, mutual understanding, intense sex sometimes, and great love always.

Developing a personal profile is the first major step that I recommend as you work to pre*fix* your marriage, and it is the subject of the next chapter. But if you're still in recovery, you cannot do that well if you haven't handled the damage that has been done in previous relationships. You wouldn't assign yourself an exercise program with multiple fractures in your leg, would you? You would wait until you've healed enough that the point of recovery could endure the pressure of exercise—or dating. For the picture you draw of yourself in an un-recovered state is vastly different than the one you will draw when you have regained, to some degree, your emotional health.

• Chapter 5 •

THE STRAIGHT TRUTH
ABOUT SELF

Or, Begin with the Beginning in Mind

P
replanning enhances our experience on most of the paths we travel, and in fact heavily influences whether or not we reach our intended destination. When we plan a summer vacation, we collect brochures, look up fun things to do on the Internet or ask others about their experiences. As we select events and locations, we figure out what to wear, what toys to take, and how to get there. When we finally book our trip we start at the beginning: which city do we fly out of? What are our budgetary constraints? How much time do we have off? What kind of experience do we seek? Journeys taken in our relational life ought to start with a similar analysis. But, because relationships do not start from a physical location, the critical components are usually not as easy to identify. As I describe some life journeys you might have experienced, notice the two pieces of information always necessary to begin.

> • First, you must know your starting point, and
> • Second, you must understand your strengths and weaknesses and current condition to assist in planning your destination.

For instance, maybe you've just taken a good look in the mirror and realized that the pounds that were silently creeping up on you have become glaringly evident. With a sigh of disgust, since this has happened several times in your life, you enroll in a weight loss program at a professional center. And speaking from my personal experience, the first session begins with an overall assessment including age, activity level, health issues, and always to my horror present weight and a "pre-diet" photo. For me, this assessment helped identify previous barriers to weight loss and helped me focus on new habits and attitudes. Much to my surprise (and relief), the healthy weight goal we identified for me at age forty was not as scary as my young twenties "ideal." Now, did you notice that the two pieces of information listed above are fully present?

> • First, the starting point was current weight and the photo, and
> • Second, strengths weaknesses, conditions of age, activity level, and health issues helped determine ideal weight.

Let's look at another short example: most graduate school applications not only require that you list previous grades and entrances exam scores, but also ask you to discuss both your strengths and potential problem areas. From this, the admissions office can get a picture of your academic profile and determine whether it is a good fit for their program. Or, consider what happens in the start-up process of a small business. Thousands of people launch businesses in North America without fully developing a business plan. This oversight has led to a stunning 70–80 percent failure rate in the first five years of operation. The other 20 percent, the successful ones, are those that engage in a full blown planning process that begins with research about themselves and their resources. They must first know their strengths and weaknesses before they can determine a "fit" in the marketplace.

The same holds true for relationships. Self-assessment is the starting point. You need to take an inventory of your unique qualities so that you will have the foundation for determining your own personal relationship journey. What we want you to do is you put yourself down on paper and get a really good look at the complete picture of you. When you start dating armed with knowledge of your own strengths and weaknesses, you've added an enormous amount of clarity to the process. You also set the stage to recognize a good fit with a potential partner as you begin dating. We must first know what we look like in order to know what we're looking for.

Steven Covey, in his bestseller *The 7 Habits of Highly Effective People*, popularized the expression "begin with the end in mind."[1] While that holds true for many things, in this instance, we back up one more planning step to say, as the sub-title of this chapter suggests, "Begin with the Beginning in Mind." The concept of understanding the importance of your present position and taking inventory of your current resources also has a rich tradition in counseling. Carl Rogers, one of the legends, grounded his mode of therapy in first taking the time to determine the "real self." Once that task is completed, then the client seeks to discover his or her "ideal self," and then the therapist and client chart a course of action that takes the client from one to the other.[2] Rogers felt that little progress could be made if initial biases and misconceptions that most people possess were not cut through to establish a secure starting point.

MIRROR, MIRROR ON THE WALL—
Shouldn't I be asking other questions?

"Wait!" you exclaim, "Are you suggesting that I may have initial misconceptions that need to be addressed as I begin this process?" The answer? Almost certainly. Recall the Garrison Keillor quote from the *Lake Wobegon* stories: "where all the women are strong, all the men are good-looking, and all the children are above average."[3] Research shows that we tend to view ourselves as better than we are. Shelley Taylor, in her 1989 book, *Positive Illusions*, finds that in North American society, approximately 80 percent of people feel they rank in the upper half of the population when they're looking at certain personal qualities. It doesn't seem to matter which quality, the principle still applies: 80 percent of people feel they're above average in attractiveness, intelligence, social skills, athletic ability, or potential for marital success. However, there is a huge problem with this.[4] Statistics offer the clinical observation that exactly 50 percent, not 80 percent, of people are above average in any given area. You can imagine how this and other misperceptions lead to unique challenges in relationships.

There are some who go about seeking Mr. Right completely unaware that they, themselves, are a walking disaster, entirely unfit for marriage. Their choice of partner makes no difference because they, themselves, will eventually destroy that relationship. And, true to what the research says, most of these "walking disasters" think they are "just fine, thank you," and can deceive many into a similar viewpoint until it is too late.

I'm sure we all have a friend like that. I remember a colleague named Clarissa who was fabulous, professional, witty, and smart looking, but each time she entered into a new relationship a similar pattern emerged. The guy would be enthralled initially, step up the pace of the romance and things would look wonderfully promising. Each time she would say, "Oh Elizabeth, he's the one!" But the moment his attention went elsewhere, such as a massive work deadline, or a family member in need, she would immediately interpret it as a decline in interest or that something was wrong. She wanted his attention every minute. First would come moodiness and hurt silences when they were together. Then she would begin making excessive phone calls and planning her activities so that she would just "happen to show up" where he was going to be. Eventually it would end with tears of anger and jealously, accusing him that he found other people and events more important than she. In the South, we call that "high maintenance." In this book we call it a fatal flaw. The tragedy was that she was convinced at the stormy and painful end of each of the failed relationships that it was "his" fault. She never considered the problem was hers. She had never done a personal assessment, so she didn't know she had a fatal flaw, one that could be fixed, but a flaw nonetheless.

While we would like to think of ourselves as good-looking and above average, the hard truth of the matter is that we need to take an impersonal, cold look at ourselves. Really, instead of asking, "Mirror, mirror on the wall, who's the fairest of them all?" we should ask that mirror "What do you see in the inner-me?" In the realm of choosing a life partner, a realistic awareness of your own personal qualities becomes mandatory because only when you know yourself well are you able to look for compatible qualities in a partner and, more importantly, understand how well these qualities might eventually blend.

So now, my friend, the fun begins! From this point forward, you can consider yourself officially started on the right path to finding a real love that will last a lifetime.

IDENTIFICATION OF PERSONAL QUALITIES

Twenty-four hundred years ago, the legendary philosopher, Socrates, identified the secret to successful living with the simple dictum "Know thyself." The words ring as true today as when he first wrote them, but how do you get to "know yourself?" How do you go about a self-assessment? My first suggestion is to write down your own personal qualities or characteristics. Now, I hear some of you arguing: "Do I actually need to write them down? Can't I just keep them in my head?" The dismal success rate of marriages suggests otherwise. Writing down qualities will not only clarify your personal characteristics but will cue your memory for other facets suggested by those you already have.

Which descriptors, then, do you write? As suggested in the previous paragraph, you want to write qualities that might influence your success in any relationship that you would share with another person. For instance, traits such as affectionate, romantic, hard working, explosive temper, critical, tall, funny, or disorganized are likely to have an influence on relationships. Hair or eye color, shoe size or your favorite food may not. The issue at this point is not whether each quality is good, bad, or neutral, but merely does it impact your relationships.

To help you create a reasonably comprehensive list of your personal qualities, I have provided two aids. One is a list of idea starters and categories that will help coach your efforts. The second is an actual example of qualities of a hypothetical person. We start with the list.

The following eleven categories give you a good idea of the kinds of qualities that are important and could influence, in some degree, your success in relationships and marriage. As you read them, start thinking about which qualities you have that fit into each of these categories. A worksheet with these headings is included at the end of this chapter. You might consider copying and enlarging it; after-all at some point it might be fun to fill it in with a boyfriend. (I used the chart with Darren early on, and he and I had a great time filling it out. We laughed a lot and enjoyed getting to know each other by going from truly important qualities to silly. It ultimately helped make our relationship stronger.)

- **Social & Relational**: e.g., extraverted, love parties, socially skilled

- **Family**: e.g., three children, divorced, love family gatherings

- **Spiritual & Philosophical**: e.g., devout Christian, atheist, daily devotions

- **Temperament & Personality**: e.g., orderly, affectionate, decisive
- **Personal Habits**: e.g., slovenly, critical, map out each day
- **Interests & Passions**: e.g., classic movies, NFL football, Morgan horses
- **Intellectual, Vocational, Financial**: e.g., lawyer, ever growing, entrepreneurial
- **Physical Characteristics**: e.g., 5'4", 185 lbs., brown hair
- **Health & Fitness**: regular exercise, smoke, eat badly, diabetic
- **Contribution & Service**: e.g., member of Rotary, teach Sunday school
- **Other**: e.g., Canadian

Now, as you think about your various personal qualities in these categories, you need to consider whether a quality is going to be important or unimportant in a relationship. Let me give you some contrasting examples that help clarify what qualifies as important. If you say: my favorite dessert is Tiramisu, that's not very important because it has little impact on a relationship. However, if you say: I am a vegetarian—that has a potentially great influence on a marriage. Here are some others: my shoe size is eight—little influence; I obsess about shoes and have two hundred pairs—great influence. I enjoy watching the Olympics on TV— little influence; I am a rabid hockey fan and have season tickets—great influence. My hair color is blond—little influence; I am a professional model—great influence. Is this helping you to get the idea?

THE SAMPLE CHART

In order to help you fill out your chart more effectively, here's the sample chart I promised you. It illustrates the qualities of Glenda, our hypothetical person. Look through and see what qualities she has written down.

Personal Characteristics Chart

Category	Change Desired	Personal Quality or Characteristic
Social & Relational		Becomes weary in large groups
	✓	Relatively poor communication skills
		Has 3 very close friends
Family		Divorced
		3 children
		Parents divorced when 15
		Family traditions are important
Spiritual & Philosophical		Methodist
		Attends church regularly
		Involved in Children's ministries
		Daily prayer and devotional time
Temperament & Personality		Tends toward introversion
		Enjoys one-on-one contacts
		Affectionate
		Adventurous
		Altruistic
	✓	Tends toward depressiveness
	✓	Angers easily
		Loyal
	✓	Bitter
	✓	Often anxious
	✓	Tends to be judgmental
		Prefers plain, functional, uncluttered
Personal Habits		Reads lots of books, particularly practical and self-help
		Maintains strict household order
		Chart continued on next page...

Category	Change Desired	Personal Quality or Characteristic
...Chart continued from previous page		
Interests & Passions		Plays piano well
		Plays viola in string ensembles
		Enjoys classic movies
		Enjoys watching Olympics
Intellectual, Vocational & Financial		Engineer
		Competent
	✓	Tends toward workaholism
		Logical thinker
		Mathematical
		Entrepreneurial
		Passionate about achieving financial success
Physical Characteristics		5'5", 130 lbs.
		7 (on a scale of 10) on attractiveness
		46 years old
		Caucasian
		Graying hair
Health & Fitness		Runs (or other types of exercise) regularly
		Emphasizes healthy eating
Contributions & Service		Member of Rotary and PTA
Other		Former alcoholic

You undoubtedly noted the check (✓) in front of certain items. The checked items represent areas that are likely to provide challenges to any relationship. One of the more helpful aspects of creating this list is that it identifies, better than any other tool, your areas for improvement or change. We all have areas that need to change, but more on that later. What I want you to do now, before you go any further in the book, is to turn to the end of this chapter and actually fill in your list. Don't worry at this point if it's complete or accurate. The rest of the chapter is devoted to helping you get that complete list. But, you have to start somewhere!

How Do You Know if Your List is Complete or Accurate?

Well done! You've just taken the first and most important step to finding your ideal mate. As I've taken many people through this process, they have found it very eye-opening to not only write down what qualities make them "them" but to really see what is important.

After you have given it your best shot, show your list to selected friends, family, or acquaintances whose judgment you trust. Tell them you are making an assessment of personal qualities with an eye to personal growth and improvement. Let them know that they are not supposed to be kind or gentle. Explain further that your goal is to create a list that is fairly complete and thoroughly honest. If you wish, tell them why you are doing this, which can help guide them in their answers as they consider what you have written.

Now, while having your friends and family help you compile your list, keep in mind that just because someone thinks or says something does not necessarily mean that they are right. In order to help you determine the validity of someone's comments, you need to apply what psychologists call "looking for similar themes from independent sources." ℞ For instance, if one person points out a quality that you think doesn't apply, you may be right. The comment may be the result of your friend's "interpretive filters." But if several people say, for instance, that you should add "hurtfully critical," to your list, even if you don't think you are that way, they're probably right and you better add it. And, if they suggest positive qualities that you have overlooked, be equally prepared to add them to your list as well. Robert Burns (1750-1796) sheds light on the value of others' opinions 230 years ago (translating from his thick Scottish dialect):

O would some Power the giver gie [give] us
To see ourselves as others see us!
It would from many a blunder free us,
And foolish notion:
What airs in dress and gait would leave us,
And even devotion![5]

In other words, if you have the power to see yourself as others see you, then you could be saved from many mistakes and foolish ideas about yourself. Take what others say about you and really look at it. If it's true, then keep it. If it just seems absolutely wrong, then toss it.

The most important part of this exercise, and sometimes the hardest, is to remain honest. Norman Anderson compiled a list of 555 personal qualities that range from very positive (sincere, honest, understanding, loyal) to very negative (malicious, dishonest, cruel, obnoxious).[6] As I noted above, we like the qualities at the positive end of the scale and tend to view ourselves as possessing them. We like to think of ourselves, in the words of Shakespeare, as "stuffed with all honorable virtues."[7] It is difficult for many people to admit that they possess some of the less desirable traits. Like the grain of sand that irritates the tender membranes of the oyster, we insulate ourselves from the painful truth. As in the pearl, we look great on the outside, but the truth, the grit of sand, remains entombed. But you and I both know that there really *are* those who are "malicious, dishonest, cruel, and obnoxious," but they never seem to view themselves that way. Typically they are certain that any problems they have are "someone else's" fault. We all have a dark side to a greater or lesser degree, and while we have been culturally conditioned to celebrate our positives and hide our negatives, not confronting that dark side weakens and usually destroys the value of this exercise.

It reminds me of the joke about the gentleman who was told by his doctor that if he wanted to live he needed an immediate operation. The operation would cost $50,000. Horrified, the man responded, "I don't have $50,000, what can I do? Are there other options?" "Sure," responded the doctor, "for fifty bucks, I'll touch up the X-rays!" If you want a successful marriage you can't "touch up the X-rays." Positive illusions don't work here. A keen awareness of reality is required.

So, considering what I have just said, and looking at the list your friends and family contributed to, I want you to revisit your list, and add whatever negative or positive traits are appropriate and true for you.

HANDLING THE NEGATIVE

Okay, you've got your list. What next? Much of what you have written is probably simply factual (For our friend Glenda, for instance: 5' 5," graying hair, divorced, entrepreneurial). There is nothing to *do* with these items, they just are. However, when you are in a dating relationship, some of these merely factual items may emerge as important in determining compatibility with your potential partner as his own descriptions and his preferences become apparent.

Other areas that you came up with, perhaps loyalty, altruism, or competence, represent strengths that will tend to enhance the likelihood of a successful marriage. For such qualities, give yourself a hearty pat on the back and continue to nurture and encourage them to develop further. But remember the check marks on Glenda's list? What I want you to do now is take another look at your list. Search it for those items that require change. Look for characteristics that no matter what type of relationship you pursued or who you might be involved with would cause interpersonal challenges. Put a check mark (✓) next to all of them. These are the qualities that not only jeopardize your chance of a good marriage but also reduce the quality and happiness of your life in general. For Glenda they include: depressive tendencies, easily angered, hostile, workaholism, often anxious, and judgmental.

In the last chapter, we discussed at length the importance of handling the damage that was caused by past negative experiences prior to thinking about dating again. The same holds true here with those personal qualities that can potentially harm future relationships. If you already know how to deal with some of the negative items (perhaps workaholism and judgmental attitude), good for you. The next step is to commit to and then start a systematic program of improvement. For those areas where you are at a loss on how to respond or what to do to improve, use the same diagnosis process I recommended to examine emotional germs. There are great self-help books out there to cover most areas: how to reduce stress in life, how to get organized, or what to do with depression. But, as I counseled you before with the issues of anger, devastation, and jealousy, if, despite significant efforts, the problems are beyond your resources take the next step and seek counseling, religious or secular. However you choose to deal with the negative parts of yourself, just know that by first recognizing what they are and then deciding to do something positive about changing them, you've taken a major step towards relationship health.

When is it Safe to Start Dating?

You may be asking yourself at this point: how far do I need to be along on self-improvement efforts to start dating? If first I need to handle my emotional germs and my negative personality traits, will I ever be ready to date? Good questions. If you wait until perfection has been achieved, you will never date or marry. If you begin dating while you still have serious problems, you are likely to ruin the relationship before it gets off the ground.

I think two factors need to be in place before you start seriously looking for your life partner: 1) Have your list completed; and 2) For each problem area, create a plan to achieve growth, and then begin to implement those plans.

Most important, you can choose to change and improve these issues. If some of you find yourself resisting the idea of personal growth, look at it this way: you must make the simple choice about whether a good marriage or a happy life is important enough to put forth the effort to change. Sometimes, change takes a lifetime, but sometimes, the effort to change—in other words the process—is just as effective as the change itself. So, even when you have areas that require further growth, and who doesn't, you're not entering into the relationship blind.

Beginning the process of changing your negative behavior has another added benefit. Remember, an ideal marriage is one in which both parties are willing to work on the relationship. As you become romantically involved, at the appropriate time, share with your partner your concerns and efforts at improvement. Not only will you gain an ally to assist in the self-improvement process, but eventually your partner may start a similar process, and that in turn could start your life-long commitment to "work on it" together.

Personal Characteristics Chart

Name: _____ Date: _____

Category	Change Desired	Personal Quality or Characteristic
Social & Relational		
Family		
Spiritual & Philosophical		
Temperament & Personality		
Personal Habits		
		Chart continued on next page...

...Chart continued from previous page		
Category	Change Desired	Personal Quality or Characteristic
Interests & Passions		
Intellectual, Vocational & Financial		
Physical Characteristics		
Health & Fitness		
Contributions & Service		
Other Areas		

* Chapter 6 *

ESSENCE QUALITIES
Understanding the Fundamental You

Taking inventory is laborious, isn't it? But the results are oh, so useful. I would even suggest it is crucial for the survival of both a business and a relationship. You find out what you have and from there you can decide what you want to keep, what needs fixing, and what you should discard. While many of us have done some sort of self-analysis, few of us have been presented with the idea that there is value in distilling the list of our personal qualities down into our essences. But, it is my premise that knowing your essences, those things that are fundamental to you, becomes a critical threshold for finding your life-mate.

Darren and I started using the truth of this fairly early on in our courtship. One of his love letters to me illustrates what I'm getting at. He wrote:

> Let me respond to things that have impressed me.
> First is a quality that we both seem to possess…
> we both seem to be able to accomplish a great
> deal (the qualities associated with the business
> woman, mathematician, logical sort) and yet we
> both possess a passion (should I say intense)
> for living, for loving, for giving that, despite
> its strength, doesn't overwhelm the practical
> side of our nature but lives in dynamic harmony
> and actually feeds it. Maybe it is the quality
> that drove us as athletes to national and world
> ranking. You speak of music and cite some
> fabulous composers and some of their classic
> works. It almost brings tears to my eyes to think
> of sharing the grandeur and power of these works
> together. I have often thought, who is there on
> earth who can share my passion, my pleasure in
> high level accomplishment, my love for the Lord,
> and my urgent desire to benefit the lives of those
> I touch? It is exciting to think of the synergy
> that could exist between us, how much more
> powerfully we could touch our world for good when
> together.

Contrast that picture with the following couple I counseled: Pauline, a determined woman, was approaching forty. She had married young, and the ages of her four children ranged from four to seventeen. Now she was headed back to school. She was excited about completing a B.A. in psychology, becoming involved in research, and applying to Ph.D. programs. Upon completion of the advanced degree, she wanted to immerse herself in counseling, research, and conducting seminars to benefit many in her world. Her husband, Gunther, was a gentle, passive soul who didn't have a job and was content to live off of government support. His philosophical perspective for contentment extended no further than "a woman, a truck, and a farm." He had dropped out of school in the tenth grade and couldn't fathom why his wife would waste her energy on all this "book learning." In fact, he quite resented the amount of time she was investing in classes and thought her place was in the home.

What do you think is the likelihood of Pauline's and Gunther's relationship surviving? It doesn't take an expert to recognize that they are totally different people. We might say that they exhibited a serious mismatch of "essence qualities." Within a year of Pauline's re-entry into the academic world, she and Gunther were divorced. Even if they had stayed together, the marriage would not have thrived. They were simply too different.

So, what is your story? I'm sure you've been in love, you've been deep into a relationship, and maybe at some point began to feel that there was less of yourself. Did you find that you had had to relinquish something fundamental in order to stay in the relationship? Was it a compromise? Or did you just rationalize that what you gave up wasn't important? It is likely, however, that one day you woke up and resented where you were and grieved the loss of yourself.

The discovery and identification of your essence qualities is some of the most important work that you will you do in terms of your future, both inside and outside of any serious relationship. In the last chapter, you started the diagnostic work of getting to know yourself with the straight truth. The purpose of the work that I'm going to ask you to do in this chapter is to really get to the positive, defining elements of who you are, fundamentally. These are the non-negotiables, the things that, if taken away, take away the very thing that makes you, you—in other words, your *essence*.

WHAT ARE ESSENCE QUALITIES?

Does a rose by any other name still smell as sweet? Of course it does! In fact neither the name nor the appearance of the beautiful petals tells us what the scent will be like. It is a one-of-a-kind fragrance, just like you are a one-of-a-kind woman. Essence qualities are the defining "contents" of our identity, those positive elements of who you are, fundamentally. The most obvious of them will be easy to identify. You will begin to look for them among the dozens of qualities you listed in your personal assessment that you created in the last chapter. While you may have listed dozens of personal characteristics, the typical individual has only eight to ten essence qualities. As you go through your personal inventory and start to think about what your essence qualities are, you may find that you identify new things that better describe your essences. If this happens to you, be sure to place them back in the larger personal characteristic list as well.

It has been my experience that distilling your list of personal qualities down to essences is a process of personal discovery, and it's likely that you may have to revisit the list over time. As Darren and I have conducted seminars through the years, we've found that it takes people a while to actually distill their list down to eight to ten essential characteristics. Even now, in my own list, I change a word here and there as I seek to capture and understand the magic of the real "me."

To help you get started, let's look at the guidelines that help you identify your own essences:

Definingly Personal: Above all, an essence quality defines who we are. These are the items that are non-negotiable; items that if you relinquish them, then you are no longer yourself. For example, one of the qualities on my list is: "I'm a 'fix-it' person." That is truly a fundamental part of who I am. I like to fix things and people, hence my career type, this book, and my company Pre*fix* Solutions Inc. In my personal life, I find myself savoring the puzzle of maintaining our computers, networking our office, and hooking up the multi-component stereo, which are activities sometimes thought of as "guy" things. In marriage, if I had to give that up, then I would no longer be the person that my husband married. Darren recognizes this and rather than be irritated or "turf" threatened, he merely grins and says, "Yeah you're good at fixing the gadgets, but I play the trombone better."

Never Negative: Essences are never negative qualities. While I encouraged you to list negative personal characteristics in the previous chapter, these can never be your essence qualities. Essence qualities are by definition positive; they must affirm who you are as a human being. It is true that there are people who are defined by their irritability, manipulative nature, explosive outbursts, general pessimism, codependency or an array of other disheartening conditions. However, we would call these negative personal traits (the ones that must either be changed or they will remain fatal to a relationship), not essence qualities. To give you an example: I used to have an explosive temper, a short fuse, but that's not an essence quality, that's a fatal flaw. While it is something I work on continuously to correct, it can never be turned around into a positive trait. While some of the negative things you identify might be characteristic of you, they are qualities or emotions that you must work actively to change in order to have a successful marriage.

Now there is a tricky part to this. There are some personality traits that may look negative but which actually contain the seeds of essences. The example I'm thinking of is a quality like bluntness. "Being blunt" might actually be negative, but you need to ask yourself if there is a constructive side. The positive aspect of bluntness could be stated as: "I am direct," and "being direct" can absolutely qualify as an essence quality.

Enduring: Essences are those qualities that are typically a part of one's identity, have been a component of one's identity for some time, and are likely to remain there well into the future, usually for a lifetime. Some contrasts may help provide clarity on what I mean: "student" is an unlikely essence; it lasts for only a limited time. "Lifetime learner" may be an essence. "Member of the PTA" probably doesn't qualify, but "contributor to society" may. "Rides roller coasters" doesn't work, but "extraverted stimulus seeker" may. Your exact measurements, "5'5" and 125 lbs," is too limited, but "devoted to lifelong fitness" might be a fundamental part of who you are. "Member of the First Baptist Church of such and such city" is too confining; "devout Christian" is a likely candidate as an essence quality.

Prompts Action: Essences are not passive, meaning they are not things that "just happen." Instead they prompt us to action in the areas of our lives that we have determined to be the most important or vital. For instance, take the idea of talent. I have a friend whose natural singing voice is unbelievably beautiful, and while she enjoys the occasional family sing-a-long, she doesn't pursue voice lessons or any other development of her talent. On the other hand, Darren and I are great friends with a student who is a voice major and governs all aspects of her life, from social activities to career, around the development and use of her voice for performance. Her essence quality of her love of music prompts her to make deliberate choices and take actions that involve her thoughts, emotions, and behaviors.

WHY ARE ESSENCE QUALITIES IMPORTANT?

Through research and experience, I believe that accurately identifying these essence qualities and matching them with those of a significant other is the single most important factor in determining compatibility and success in your marriage. Let me repeat that: *matching essence qualities is the single most important factor in determining compatibility between two persons considering marriage.* So, in order to really determine if you are compatible with someone, you must start with the step of identifying and understanding your own essences. When you are thoroughly acquainted with yours and the dynamics of how they related to your life, then we can move to the next step of determining a match based on essences. But be patient, that's still a few chapters away.

At the personal level, it is important to focus on and even attempt to enhance essence qualities. As mentioned earlier, essence qualities are simply the fundamental, defining "contents" of our personal identity. Those with a weak identity and a general dearth of essences tend to live vague passive lives without direction and with little meaning. Research reveals that those with weak identities (hence lack of essence qualities) suffer lower self-esteem, experience more depression, are less successful financially, exhibit poorer emotional stability, and reveal a variety of other deficits. And none of these traits make for a happy marriage; for as detrimental as the lack of essences is to an individual, it is even more damaging when attempting to form relationships.

 One of the legends of developmental psychology was a man named Erik Erickson. Despite having never finished a college degree (not even a B.A.) the influence of his theories to the psychological world is enormous. He proposed the eight stages of psychosocial development that described critical developmental tasks at different phases of life. Our interest relates only to the fifth, the identity stage, and the sixth, the intimacy stage, of his theory.[1]

Erickson argues that stage five, the "identity" stage, ideally forms during the teen and early adult years (roughly puberty through mid-twenties). The primary function of these years is to form a reasonably secure identity. This includes understanding our values and our roles, finding a likely professional path, and painting some sort of picture of what one would like to accomplish during one's sojourn on this earth. This stage needs to be relatively complete before we seriously consider stage six. Erickson calls stage six the "intimacy" stage and it involves forming a committed intimate relationship with someone of opposite sex, usually a marriage. During the 1960s, while Erickson was a professor at UC Berkeley, he spent much of his time proposing that the major problem with today's society was the reversal of stages five and six. For instance, it is not uncommon today for thirteen and fourteen year olds to become sexually involved before they have even a clue as to who they are. The divorce rate when both partners are teen-agers at the time of marriage? An appalling 90 percent. Darren and I are fully supportive of Erickson's ideas. If you have little to no identity, if you don't know who you are, how can you possibly have the perspective to determine whether a relationship can work? Therefore, while this chapter is concerned with identifying your essence qualities, know that it is also vital to your future relationships that you strengthen any essence qualities that are weak.

The Stronger the Adherence to Essences the Stronger the Individual

Soon, you're going to start the process of listing out your essence qualities. In order to assist you further in this process, I'm going to take a moment and look at one of the great men in American history. On July 4, 2005, *Time* magazine came out with a special issue on Abraham Lincoln. Numerous articles devoted to his story took up thirty-eight pages of the magazine. One of the articles was "The Master of the Game" by renowned historian, Doris Kearns Goodwin. It was an excellent and inspiring article, and Goodwin actually identified the qualities Lincoln possessed that made him so great, and as I read them I realized that the list likely reflected his personal essences. Here they are:

Empathy: This ranks as the most important of Lincoln's qualities; the ability to put himself in the place of another and to experience their world from their perspective. Even as a child it is said that he was exceptionally tenderhearted. He once tracked back half a mile to rescue a pig caught in the mire. Rather than castigating the Southern states he made efforts to understand their perspective. In his second inaugural address, March 4, 1865, as the war was drawing to a close, Lincoln illustrated his empathy and compassion: "With malice toward none, with charity for all, with firmness in the right as God gives us to see the right, let us strive on to finish the work we are in; to bind up the nation's wounds, to care for him who shall have borne the battle and for his widow and orphan." [2]

Humor: Humor was intrinsic to Lincoln. An old-timer who frequently observed the President, described him telling jokes: "When he began telling one, his eyes would sparkle with fun and when he reached the point in his narrative which invariably evoked the laughter of the crowd, nobody's enjoyment was greater than his." [3] Lincoln used humor to relieve tensions, to mend relationships, and to illustrate a point of view that might be awkward to present directly. This was one of his favorite stories: Shortly after the peace was signed, the Revolutionary War hero, Ethan Allen, had occasion to visit England where he was subjected to teasing banter. The British would make fun of the Americans and General Washington in particular and one day they got a picture of General Washington and displayed it prominently in the outhouse so Allen could not miss it. When he made no mention of it, they finally asked him if he had seen the Washington picture. Allen said he thought that it was a very appropriate place for an Englishman to keep it. "Why?" they asked. "For," said Mr. Allen, "there is nothing that will make an Englishman s—

so quick as the sight of General Washington." [4] A little off-color? Maybe, but funny, certainly, and Lincoln's ability to find humor in any situation helped a nation during its darkest hour.

Magnanimity: Lincoln refused to bear grudges. He refused to acknowledge a slight. Early in his career Edwin Stanton called Lincoln "a long-armed ape" and declined to relate to him at any level. After Lincoln was elected President, he appointed Stanton his Secretary of War because, as Lincoln put it, "Stanton was the best man for the job." Stanton was at Lincoln's bedside when he died and was the man who uttered the immortal phrase, "Now he belongs to the ages." [5]

Generosity of spirit: When someone under Lincoln's command was justly criticized, Lincoln would often take the blame himself and absolve the one being attacked. He also allowed others to share the limelight. After several dramatic victories, Ulysses S. Grant was being honored in Washington. Lincoln stepped aside and allowed Grant to enjoy the place of honor that was typically accorded the President. Furthermore, when Lincoln was wrong, he admitted it readily.

Perspective: Lincoln always made sure to keep a sense of perspective, to look at events in context of what was happening around them. This story illustrated this point best. Early in the war, Lincoln met at the home of George McClellan, general of the Union army, to discuss urgent matters concerning the war. Lincoln's secretary, John Hay, described what happened. McClellan was at a wedding and when he returned (knowing that Lincoln was waiting) he bypassed the room Lincoln and Hay were in. A half hour later, a servant informed the president that McClellan had gone to bed. Hay was furious. Lincoln's response, recorded in Hay's diary was: "Lincoln seemed not to have noticed it specially, saying it was better at this time not to be making points of etiquette and personal dignity." [6]

Whether it was Stanton calling him a "damned fool" or Grant's excessive drinking, Lincoln realized there were larger issues at stake and made use of his legendary humor to soften the tension. In response to Stanton's reported comment, Lincoln responded: "If Stanton said I was a damn fool, then I must be one, for he is nearly always right and generally says what he means. I will step over and see him." Reports of Grant's drinking surfaced after several major Union victories and Lincoln responded: "If you can find the brand of whisky Grant uses, I will distribute it at once to the rest of his generals." [7]

Self control: As Goodwin described: "When angry at someone, Lincoln would occasionally write a hot letter, but then would invariably put it aside until he had cooled down, at which point he no longer needed to send it." If he did lose his temper in public it was followed with an immediate, heartfelt apology. His most severe test was when General Meade, following victory at Gettysburg, allowed Lee's army to get away, effectively prolonging the war by another two years. Lincoln wrote a letter to Meade in which he said that he was "distressed immeasurably by the magnitude of the misfortune." Realizing the great pain such a letter would cause the general he put the letter in an envelope and wrote, "To Gen. Meade, never sent or signed." [8]

A sense of balance: Lincoln understood Steven Covey's concept of "sharpen the saw," to take time to for yourself to improve yourself. During the war, when many in government or the military would work themselves far beyond exhaustion, Lincoln realized the importance of allowing time to regroup and to recuperate. The manager of Grover's Theater in Washington estimated that Lincoln had attended more than a hundred times during his presidency. It allowed him for a few moments to forget the war and refresh his spirits.

A social conscience: Lincoln wanted above all else to accomplish something worthy that would stand the test of time. Lincoln suffered severe depression at two times in his life, when he was twenty-six and thirty-two. So profound was his misery that his friends feared suicide. When Lincoln was confronted with their fears he acknowledged that in many ways he wished to die, but stated that "I have done nothing to make any human being remember that I have lived . . . to link my name with something that redounds to the interest of my fellow man is what I desire to live for. I must leave the world a little better for my having lived in it." [9] Clearly this remained a driving force throughout his life.

CREATING YOUR OWN LIST

R̥

Okay, now that you've been inspired by Lincoln, it's time to turn your attention to your own list. At the end of this chapter, there is a blank worksheet. To start honing your list of essence qualities, do these following steps:

1. Look at the list from your Personal Characteristics in the chapter 5 on "The Straight Truth About Self." Put an asterisk (*) by as many items as you think most represent you, the ones you can't live without.

2. Now, we're going to test each one. As you consider each asterisked item, think back to the guidelines for determining essence qualities earlier in the chapter and ask:

- Is it definingly personal?
- It is non-negotiable (meaning, without it you're no longer you)?
- Is it stated in the positive?
- Is it enduring?
- Does it prompt you to action?
- Can it be taken away and you could still stand it?

If your item fails any of these questions, it's not an essence quality. It's still part of your personal inventory, but it is something that can be modified, or deleted, and you would still be you.

As you begin this exercise, try to identify those things you feel at the deepest gut level. For example, in my case, you could take cooking or shopping off of the face of the earth and I would be fine, but don't you dare touch my music!

Once you have honed your list, transfer those qualities that have passed this test to the sheet at the back of this chapter. As you do this, try to group them in order of strength and importance. Place those that have the greatest capacity to define you at the top. Don't worry if the grouping is not totally accurate, particularly as you first begin to consider these things. As you contemplate this idea, you will develop a better sense of yourself as well as become more articulate in being able to relate to others who you are and what makes you tick.

THE JOYOUS SELF-EXPRESSION OF ESSENCES

As you work on finding your essences, know that above all, essence qualities are important because they provide avenues for joyous self-expression. You'll remember that I told you that I wouldn't be able to stand it if you took away my music. When I first met Darren, I was singing in a choir; he played piano and trombone. We knew that we both had a great love for music, but the way I engaged in it wasn't as compatible with Darren as it could be. So, at age forty, I decided to learn to play an instrument with which to accompany Darren on the trombone. I selected the horribly cantankerous, bone-meltingly beautiful French horn. Today, we weave the lovely tones of the trombone and horn together, much like the caressing of fingers in public. But in my heart of hearts, my most precious moments with the horn are those when I play by candlelight in the privacy of my home, and my soul blends with the music and flows into the silent places of the night. My essence blends with his essence, but it also brings me pure joy.

What I hope you find, as you complete this exercise, is an increasing excitement as you develop a keener sense of your purpose and meaning. Know that essence qualities are there to grow, but you cannot change them without doing grave harm to yourself. You may want to enhance them, even pursue them. You definitely want to embrace them, but as the song said from the 1970s: "don't go changing, to try 'n please me" [10] You are a beautiful human being who has much to offer, and as you think about this chapter and hone your list of essence qualities, think of them as precious gifts to be shared.

Individual Essence Qualities Worksheet

Name: _____ Date: _____

Note: List qualities of greater strength or importance toward top

Essence Qualities

STEP TWO OF THE PRE*fix* PROCESS

Take a Look Outward

EQUIPPING YOURSELF WITH PROPER TOOLS AND ARMOR

At the end of chapter 1, I told you that in order to marry successfully, you need to start with the right blueprint. You need the right model and set of rules, and you need to hunt in the right forest. Now that you've done some work on yourself—you've identified your strengths and weaknesses and you've put in place steps to at least start handling the germs from past relationships—you might be thinking that you're ready to start dating again.

Trust me, you're not. If you've experienced one or more broken relationships, and are contemplating going out with someone, it is most likely you feel vulnerable. Pay attention to that feeling because it's warning you to stop and take this second, very important step, "Taking a Look Outward." It is the interim stage of the pre*fix* process. This step equips you with knowledge. As you create your image of compatibility it will help you recognize the right individual when you see him. In addition it provides you with armor so that not only will you recognize those "don't date this guy" warnings, but will also prepare you to defend against those things that will sabotage your search.

To help you understand just how important this step is, I'm going to give you a model we use in Human Resource Management. Remember, I'm an HR person by training, and in the business world, I'm the person who helps management decide who they should hire and why. As I've counseled people through their personal relationships, I've always been struck by the similarity in the processes of staffing for the organization versus dating for the marriage. If you're in business, you know that it's bad policy to go about the hiring process in a reckless manner. In HR, when there is a need for a position to be filled, we go through a series of steps that help us get ready to find the right person for the job. When you are beginning to date, you are, essentially, looking for the best man to fill the job, so both in HR and in finding your perfect life partner, you begin by first conducting a job analysis. You do an analysis of internal characteristics, just like we did in "Step One: Take a Look Inward." In a business, this step helps you look at the mission of the organization and determine what jobs are needed, which need changing, and which need eliminating. In preparing yourself for dating, you looked at your personal characteristics and determined what you have and from there you decided what you want to keep, what needs fixing, and what you should discard. But in HR, just because we've done that, we're still not ready to place a want ad, just as you are not yet ready to go dating.

We next identify what the candidate should be able to do and what qualifications/credentials they need to have in order to do it. In HR, this is called the job description (what makes up the job, the things required to do it) and job specification, the credentials and qualifications of the candidate that show he or she is able to do the task outlined in the description. This is essentially what you are going to do here in Step Two. You're first going to draw a picture of your ideal candidate. Then, you're going to identify those things that would disqualify him as your life partner, and finally you are going to identify those areas that could potentially sabotage your rational thinking during the process of dating. This last step, in the HR analogy I'm using here, is arming yourself with a knowledge of the legalities. It is not wise, for instance, to base your hiring decisions merely on the candidate's good looks (unless you're a modeling agency), and you need to find out what all the legal "no-no's" are before you start your search process. In a dating situation, you need to know what things can cloud your judgment. While they aren't illegal, these things are based on emotion. You need to be aware and armed with the knowledge of those things that can undermine you from making a rational decision.

Effective job analysis is essential to sound human resource management, and there is a direct parallel to the dating process as you define your ideal partner, select him, and then work to grow your marriage. As we move forward from looking inward at ourselves to this next step, we begin to consider what fits and what doesn't, but we also must know what we want and what we don't want before we make the jump back into the forest and begin our hunt. Hunting, while it can be dangerous, can also be loads of fun. It's what we do when we shop; we hunt for the perfect outfit—and shoes, of course. I must warn you, however. While the first part of this section is interesting to do as well as instructive, the rest of it requires you to take a hard look at what you don't like. And know this, if you don't do the processes that are outlined in these chapters in a reasonably complete fashion, it will have negative implications on the likelihood of your future success in marriage.

So, even though I've given you a bunch of different metaphors in this introduction to Step Two, from HR to hunting, I'm going to stick with shopping. Not only is shopping fun, I couldn't help but think of what I take with me every time I go on a shopping trip and how suitable each item is to each chapter in this section. Anytime I go shopping, I have my list, pepper spray, and a can of almonds. Why? Because, my list keeps me focused, the spray ensures that I will be able to get rid of the undesirables—something you always want to have when you're shopping for a man—and my can of almonds keeps me full if I'm hungry so that I'm not tempted to buy things I shouldn't, like high-carb foods full of sugar which may look great and taste yummy, but they don't feed my body well. Just like all those men who look great but in the long run won't satisfy your emotional needs.

• Chapter 7 •

YOUR IDEAL OTHER

*How to Prepare for One of the Most
Important Shopping Trips of Your Life*

Have you ever watched the difference between the way men and women shop? Men tend to be direct. They know what they want beforehand. They walk into a store, go right to the place where they might find it, and if what they want isn't there, they leave. Women tend to do something I call entertainment shopping. They like the whole experience of shopping, the sights, the smells, the various interactions between people. Well, my friends, you are about to go shopping, and while what I just gave you is a gross generalization, the two categories are instructive.

I happen to be more man-like in my shopping habits. I get an image of what I need or want—the suit complete with shoes and accessories. I even take my color swatches with me so I know which colors make me look good as well as having my fabric samples and my paint colors from my living room so that if I need to match colors and textures, I can.

Consequently, my colors are coordinated; I don't have random things in my closet or in my house. Whether it is my shoes, my skin color, or my couch, everything I buy is going to match what it needs to match. This is called planned shopping.

Both men and women can be entertainment shoppers. The browsing itself, in a dating situation, is a recreational or social pursuit, and there is nothing wrong with browsing, per se. The problem comes when the casual shopper ends up being attracted to something and spontaneously buys it, but that thing—whether it be an electronic toy, a purse, or a partner—is totally out of context with their life. Maybe it was too good of a deal to pass up. Maybe, you thought it would be a great gift for some friend in the future. But, someday, that thing that you just *had to have* usually ends up being a garage sale or a donation-box item, or…a broken heart. Now, I'm not here to tell you that you can't indulge in some entertainment shopping when it comes to men. It's sometimes fun to try different varieties. But, that's not the purpose of this book. You picked this book up because you wanted guidance on how to go about finding the right mate for you in the right way. So, when you're searching for a life partner, know that you are going on a planned shopping trip. Just like I know what colors, cut, style, and size I need in a suit, you too will have, by the end of this chapter, a more grounded idea of what you are looking for in a partner.

If some of you are groaning because you think we are taking out the romance and that having a list is too boring or stodgy, or even too "pre-planned," keep in mind that something really interesting happens when you know what you're looking for. In marketing terms it's called selective exposure, where we seek out and notice only information that interests us. It's the phenomenon that happens when, say, you just bought a pair of Ralph Lauren sunglasses or a brand new Toyota Camry, and all of a sudden, everyone is wearing your type glasses or driving your type car! Once we focus our attention on a subject, we then notice it in our environment. It happens to pregnant women all the time. You find out your going to have a baby and you notice pregnant women all over the place. What happened to me was even funnier: I don't remember ever meeting a twin until I had my girls and then I found twins everywhere!

If we envision what we want, we're more likely to find it because we will recognize it when we see it. That's the whole purpose of this chapter: you get to build your very own and very realistic "Mr. Right," and you do it based on all the work that you did in the previous chapters. And, once you have your ideal other described, when you do start searching, you'll start recognizing what you like and don't like. You might see a sexy hunk and think "yummy," but you look at his personal qualities and say, "might look good but it doesn't fit with my colors. Next."

Now, let me caution you what this chapter isn't about. This chapter isn't going to have you write an exhaustive list of everything that you want in a man. That is as disastrous as not having a list at all because you'd never find someone who matches everything that you desire. Anyone who creates an exhaustive list and begins the equally exhausting search for the perfect other is facing the impossible. The list is meant as your guide. It gives you some parameters so you keep focused on the task at hand.

DRAFTING YOUR IDEAL LIST

The way that you figure out what "Mr. Right" really looks, feels, and acts like is straightforward. You are going to use a chart that looks like the ones that you used to generate your personal characteristics and then your essence qualities, and, on the blank chart, you're going to have some fun writing down the qualities you would like in your ideal other. As you continue through this chapter you will see the value of writing them down. Once your list is reasonably complete, keep it handy—in today's computer age, that usually means saving it in some file on your computer—and pull it out from time to time to refresh your memory. Better yet, put it on your fridge to keep you focused and on track.

Just like your other worksheet on your personal characteristics, this one is divided into eleven areas: social and relational, family, spiritual/philosophical, temperament/personality, personal habits, interest and passions, intellectual/vocational, physical, health and fitness, contributions and service, and other areas, but on this chart, there is an additional column for you to code the importance of these qualities. After you have written down a number of qualities that you want in your ideal other, you are then going to code each quality on the four-point scale I list on the next page. Fill in the blanks without a lot of worry about whether what you put is appropriate or not. What is important about the coding is that it will help you sort out whether a particular item is urgent to whether it's merely the icing on the cake.

Here's the scale:

1 = Required—something your future mate must have. If the quality is not present it's a "deal breaker."

2 = Highly desirable—not required but greatly desired

3 = Desirable—an enjoyed quality but you're willing to be flexible

4 = Preference—nice if it is there, but no problem if it isn't

To give you an idea of what this all looks like, below is a profile of qualities created by a hypothetical woman who is in search of a partner. In this list we have organized the entries so that the most important items are at the start of each section.

My Ideal Other

Catgory	Personal Quality or Characteristic	Coding
Social & Relational	Excellent communication skills	2
	Enjoyably but not excessively social	3
Family	Close family ties	1
	Wants an open home—all who come feel welcome	2
	Loves children (and wants children)	2
Spiritual & Philosophical	Committed Christian	1
	Pays tithe (10 percent of income) to support the church and ministries	1
	Belongs to my denomination	2
	Actively involved in church ministries	3
Temperament & Personality	Affectionate	1
	Confident	2
	Good sense of humor	2
	Gentle	2
	Adaptable, able to be influenced (not stupidly stubborn)	2
	Emotionally healthy	2
	Adventurous	3
	Chart continued on next page…	

...Chart continued from previous page		
Personal Habits	Commitment to ever growing	1
	Non-smoker	1
	Non (or moderate) drinker	2
	Non materialistic	2
	Neat and orderly	2
Interests & Passions	Loves music (and types of music we enjoy mesh well)	2
	Loves the outdoors	2
	Enjoys classic movies	3
	Loves (and wants) pets	4
	Plays piano well	4
Intellectual, Financial	Intelligent	1
	Able to think logically	1
	A profession that meshes well with mine	2
	Eager to build toward financial abundance	2
	Learns from mistakes and applies knowledge to future success	2
Physical Characteristics	Personally appealing (face, hair, build)	1
	5' 10" (± 4")	2
	155 lbs. (± 20 lb.) (lean, athletic build)	2
	Older than me	3
	Hispanic	4
Health & Fitness	Committed to high level of fitness	1
	Regular exercise schedule	1
	Vegetarian	3
	Runs in road races	4
Contributions & Service	Wishes to achieve wealth primarily to benefit worthy causes	2
	Cares for those less fortunate	2
	Involved in an active form of service to his community	2

As you read through this, note that our hypothetical person rating her sweetie has a limited number of items coded "1." If you have too many "1s" you will probably never find a match. Allow flexibility as you create your list. The "1s" represent core items that you keep your eye out for; those coded lower ("2s," "3s", and "4s") represent negotiables.

Let's explore how powerful this list really is to you. I lightly touched on it above, but there's something deeper going on. Psychologist Maxwell Maltz found that when a person has a clear image of any desired object or goal in mind that is frequently remembered and reviewed, the subconscious mind will automatically begin the search for a match to correspond with that image.[1] In fact most motivational experts emphasize that the most powerful methods of achieving a goal is twofold: 1) the goal must be clearly defined and written down; and 2) that goal must be consciously examined, visualized, and experienced. This process, says Maltz, will unleash the power of your subconscious to eventually realize that goal. There is no questioning the validity and power of this procedure. People have used these visualization techniques to become better athletes, scholars, and speakers. It has even been used to earn more money. Why not use this powerful tool to find a suitable marriage partner?

Note that while the procedure is beneficial, there may not be anyone who actually matches on all points that you visualize. But the important qualities will become deeply rooted in your subconscious and a more valid search will ensue than if you are just vaguely looking for something opposite-sexed, attractive, and fun. Having the image will also help protect you from returning to the default setting in your mind where the scripts from the fairy-tale model kick in.

So now, it's your turn. I'm sure as you were reading this chapter, you were thinking about what you would like to have in your ideal mate. Now is the time to write them down and make your wishes known! Worry about coding them after you get a reasonably complete list.

How to Use Your Ideal List

Once you have your profile, it is important to keep a few guidelines in mind as you start searching. Remember that the purpose of this process is to create an overall picture. It is designed to give you an image so that when you meet someone you'll recognize a potential fit more quickly. This is not a grocery list of individual elements that you tick off. That type of thinking would be confining and doomed to failure. It is unrealistic to think that one individual will have everything on your list, and of equal importance you want to be open to previously un-thought of possibilities. In all likelihood, when you do find your life mate, he will have wonderful characteristics that had never occurred to you.

Now that this information is in place, it is not necessary to obsess about it. Review it from time to time, particularly noting the items that were coded ones and twos. It is vital to have the ideas firmly planted in your mind. Once there in your subconscious, they will serve a useful function in all your interactions with other available people. In a casual setting you might encounter someone who has important qualities that you desire in a mate. If so, you might determine some way to introduce yourself and get to know him better. If you go on a date, evidence may emerge that indicates whether or not a second date is warranted. What we're steering you away from is those impulse reactions. We don't want you to have to rely on instinct and impulse as you select a future mate. The 95 percent failure rate of instant romances and quick marriages verify that impulse is a very poor mechanism for selecting a partner.

As you think about your list and write down various qualities and revise it, there's a final thought I want to share. One of my closest friends has experienced several failed relationships. As she talked with me about what she needed and wanted in her significant other, we both realized that her list had changed over time. Her movement through different life stages had generated some of the changes; the school of hard knocks had caused others. So be open. If you had a fixed idea when you were younger of what kind of mate you wanted and this list is shaping up as something different, that's okay. What was ideal for you, as a young never-been-in-a committed-relationship woman, is probably different now as well. The important thing to remember is that, like your list of personality traits and essence qualities, this list isn't usually generated in one sitting. Spend some time over the next few months working on your ideal. Revise as needed, but remember that the relationship you paint with this exercise will be a huge source of influence on your future happiness and satisfaction. I encourage you to use hindsight, blend it with foresight and create an image that will help you "see" your ideal partner when you meet him. This is not the same as love at first sight; instead, it is recognizing qualities that you have identified as important that warrant getting a closer look.

And don't forget to have some fun doing this. Think of it like the way we used to approach creative projects in grade school. Our fingers

100 • THE COMPATIBILITY CODE

would be thick with paint and we were allowed to smear, throw, do almost whatever we liked with it (eating it was usually not a good idea); we were never stopped by cynicism. Our images were created from abandonment, not restraint. Create! Have fun, and don't limit yourself. The picture you paint is very likely what you will find, so always be open to the bigger possibilities.

My Ideal Other

Name: _____ Date: _____

Category	Personal Quality or Characteristic	Coding
Social & Relational		
Family		
Spiritual & Philosophical		
Temperament & Personality		
Personal Habits		
	Chart continued on next page...	

...Chart continued from previous page		
Interests & Passions		
Intellectual, Vocational & Financial		
Physical Characteristics		
Health & Fitness		
Contributions & Service		
Other Areas		

* Chapter 8 *

So—What Breaks the Deal?

Warning: No Romance
Found in This Chapter!

Well my friends, I hope that you had a marvelous time figuring out what your ideal "Mr. Right" looks like on paper. You've got a great image in your mind, but, again, I warn you against embarking on your search just yet. It's like this: if you had a crystal ball, you could see everything there was to know about this person that you're interested in before the first date, the first kiss, the first blossoming into romance. If you could see the full positive and negative profile of this individual, your common sense would more than likely protect you from making the wrong decision. But you don't have a crystal ball nor do you have any early-warning indicators in your arsenal to protect you from getting into the wrong relationship. In other words, you don't have your relationship pepper-spray primed and ready to go. While you have good intentions for finding the ideal someone who fleshes out what you've put on paper, the very thing that is going to protect you from undesirables is not yet primed and ready for action.

When it comes to stuff—the material things in life—we are usually not afraid to walk away from something because it doesn't fit with what we were looking for. If the item we are considering has even a single flaw that renders it unusable, you simply don't purchase it. Say you go out to buy a pair of dress shoes. You find the finest looking pair of shoes this side of the Mississippi. You fall in love immediately but discover that the shoes are size seven; you wear size eight. No purchase, end of discussion. Say you are pregnant and go out to buy a mommy-mobile. You find a 1957 Ford Thunderbird. You have dreamed of owning such a vehicle all your life. But the Thunderbird (at least the 1957 version) seats only two. It's not practical and isn't what you need so, painful as it may be you let it go and continue searching for a minivan. We are even savvier when we see flaws in merchandise such as a blouse with a snag or a jacket with a stain on the arm. We know to look for such problems and put the object back on the shelf.

This is true for most of your major life-decisions as well. You're job-hunting for a middle-level management position. The job must provide $4,500 per month to fulfill the needs of your family. You are offered the perfect job. Love the boss, great location, the firm comes highly recommended and provides opportunity for personal and professional growth. It pays only $2,900 monthly. You turn down the offer and continue to look for a position that meets your financial needs. During the search for a university to pursue a career in Aerospace Engineering you find the perfect school, highly ranked in *US News and World Report*, reasonable tuition, a reputation for academic excellence, a track record of placing 98 percent of their graduates in desirable positions. They don't have a program in aerospace engineering. End of discussion, you look elsewhere.

What I'm talking about are those things that can break a deal. In our seminars, we call them "deal-breakers" or "disqualifiers," because if you come up against one of them in the process of dating (or buying a car or deciding on a college) they disqualify the item in question.

Disqualifiers are usually obvious in consumer products; but up to this point, we generally haven't considered using them to prevent a non-fit in relationships. So, within the context of human relationships let us define a disqualifier as, "*a quality or characteristic of another person that eliminates them from being considered as a potential marriage partner.*" In simplest terms, if someone has such a quality, even one, you will not marry him. When it comes to the material aspects of life, deal-breakers are much easier to determine and make decisions about because you usually have little if any emotional attachment. But, let's face it. We're not usually willing to be so bold in our decision making process when it comes to finding the right guy. But since you don't want to be wearing the wrong man at your wedding, we need to get a little brutal in our thinking about potential mates.

Unfortunately, in present society the disqualifiers of a potential partner are often overlooked for two reasons:

1. We don't know that disqualifiers exist or have not identified them, or
2. We are so emotionally involved with a person that we try to make it work despite disqualifiers.

℞

Because we've shopped for material items most of our lives, we know what types of fit or flaw problems prevent purchase. In the context of thinking about whether or not to date someone we don't have the same level of experience or knowledge about things that truly doom relationships. Additionally, if we could stand back and be impartial—devoid of the many emotional factors—saying "no" to a potential date would be as straightforward as putting the shoes that don't fit back on the shelf. The purpose of this chapter is really two-fold. I want to help you develop the right set of disqualifiers, and I want to help get you into the right mindset about using them. I'm not going to sugarcoat this one, though. The mindset that I want you to take possession of is this: when you come across a disqualifier in a potential partner, you will not compromise, period. You end the relationship. Brutal? Yes. Unromantic? Absolutely. Necessary? You can bet the rest of your happily married life on it.

How to Identify a Disqualifier or Deal-breaker ℞

That sounds neat and clean, but we all know that life is not generally neat or clean. Sometimes disqualifiers are crystal clear. For instance, I would not marry anyone who smokes. No ambiguity there: if they smoke, even one cigarette a day, I would not even date them, let alone marry them. Usually, though, disqualifiers are not nearly so obvious. Here's an example: "I will not marry someone who is critical." While this is a great choice for a disqualifier, how do you define "critical"? Is one critical comment per year okay? How about one per month, one per week, one per day? In a bit, I'm going to ask you to create your list of disqualifiers. It is desirable, as you do that exercise, to consider the consequences of disqualifiers to yourself and your future marriage if you did choose a person with such a trait. But before you really hunker down and do this unpleasant but necessary work, let me give you some insight and examples about two categories of disqualifiers: those from research and those that are personally determined.

First I'll present those characteristics that psychological research has identified as disqualifiers. Remember back to the work I had you do checking for your own emotional germs from previous relationships and for personal characteristics that could harm any relationship? This is a similar step, except now it is applied to the guy that wants to ask you out on a date.

 Disqualifiers from Psychological Research

Most of the personal qualities from psychological research are associated with characteristics that have been shown to be particularly destructive in essentially any relationship. You can actually look at all of these negative personal factors in the same way that you viewed your own undesirable personal qualities. These are characteristics that no matter what type of relationship you pursue would cause interpersonal challenges and greatly jeopardize your chance of a good marriage. And if you don't believe me, stop and think about it. If you decide to marry a man who consistently exhibits hostility, no matter how promising other features might be, what do you think your marriage will be like? The following list then includes people who are:

- **Hostile** (in time, it destroys everything it touches) [1]
- **Bitter** (eventually tears down self and others) [2]
- **Selfish** (a good marriage is based on give and take and understanding another's perspective) [3]
- **Rigid/uncompromising** (successful marriage requires mutual influence and compromise) [4]
- **Tactless** (causes the start-up of many an argument) [5]

- **Egotistical** (successful marriage encourages a focus on the benefit of the other) [6]

- **Controlling** (doesn't allow for necessary change and mutual influence) [7]

- **Dishonesty** (cuts the foundation out of any relationship) [8]

- **Cruel** (too much abuse in the world already) [9]

- **Poor communication skills** (communication IS the relationship and must be nurtured) [10]

- **Manipulative** (a combination of controlling, dishonest, and selfish: damages everything in its path) [11]

- **Reactive thinker** (knee-jerk, impulse-driven responses undercut successful relationships) [12]

- **Emotionally unstable** (eliminates conditions necessary for long-term forward progress) [13]

- **Overly sensitive** (a certain toughness is required to weather the challenges of marriage) [14]

- **Excessive dependency** (the "codependent" will suck energy and pleasure out of a relationship) [15]

- **Severe psychological disorders** (a cancer that eventually destroys the whole person) [16]

- **Uncontrolled anger** (often inflicts permanent damage on spouse and children) [17]

- **Habitually critical** (twenty criticisms a day for forty years equals 292,000 criticisms over a married lifetime—enough to mutilate or destroy) [18]

- **Obsessive or compulsive behavior** (absence of control pervades and destroys) [19]

Disqualifiers that are Personally Determined

While the concept of disqualifiers is rooted in psychological research, the particular items that you identify as deal-breakers are largely individual. For instance, social drinking may be a disqualifier for John but not for Sally. An atheist would probably be an unacceptable choice for a devout Christian but for someone else it might represent a good fit. What then is the source of the personally-determined disqualifier list?

The qualities or behaviors that might be identified as disqualifiers for a particular person are as diverse as the people themselves. However, there are certain traits that people commonly list as disqualifiers. In one of Darren's studies, surveying six hundred individuals in the central Alberta area, the participants were asked to share characteristics that represented to them such a violation of their personal values that anyone who possessed them would be disqualified for further consideration as a romantic partner.

To help you get started on your own list, I'm providing you with the top twenty-five items of over one hundred disqualifiers that participants identified. Here's the list, and they are rank ordered from the most frequently cited to least frequently cited. Notice that six of the items duplicate disqualifiers from psychological research. Others are just individual preferences.

1. Substance abuse
2. Smokes
3. Non-Christian
4. Lazy/unmotivated/lacking ambition
5. Unemployed or financially challenged
6. Sexually promiscuous
7. Unsanitary
8. Abusive
9. Dishonest
10. Unintelligent
11. Physically unattractive
12. From a different denomination
13. Drinks
14. Lacks humor
15. Overweight
16. Dislikes children
17. Selfish
18. Controlling
19. Antisocial

20. Doesn't share similar interests

21. Disrespectful

22. Proud/egotistical

23. Antagonism from friends and family

24. Explosive anger

25. Pessimistic

Interesting, aren't they? Keep your thinking cap on, though, because while these are a start, they aren't necessarily unique to you.

CREATING YOUR OWN LIST OF DISQUALIFIERS

As you create your list of disqualifiers, you need to include all of the psychologically based disqualifiers. Again, if that sounds harsh, just know that these characteristics are what research has shown severely jeopardize a marriage. You may also have selections from the personally-determined list, just described above. Additionally, there will be disqualifiers that are uniquely your own, things that aren't on either list.

Now, this isn't to say that we haven't developed a set of disqualifiers over the years; we just need to make sure that it is up to date and based on sound thought, not just an eclectic collection from your fairy-tale years and the school of hard knocks. And for most of you, I'm sure that you have some very strong ideas of what you can't endure in a person. In fact, I bet that most of you, as you've been reading, have already started listing in your mind your own set of disqualifiers.

I provide a worksheet at the end of the chapter to write your disqualifiers down. As a starting point, the psychological disqualifiers are already included. I've put them there because you must have them on your list. From the personally determined group, the easiest-to-pick items will be those that describe unhealthy characteristics. Through your personal experiences, you know what you can and cannot stand in person, what is acceptable and what is unacceptable. However, be aware, as you work on your personal additions to the list, make efforts to determine whether a particular characteristic is absolutely a deal-breaker or just an irritation. For the reality is that all of us have experienced many of these negative qualities at one time or another. From time to time all of us have felt or expressed hostility, have been selfish, rigid, tactless, dishonest and a host of others.

The disqualifiers that are more difficult to identify are those items that merely represent important differences as opposed to unhealthy traits. For instance, one of my disqualifiers is someone who doesn't actively enjoy and support the classical arts. The subject of the arts isn't positive or negative, it is neither a healthy nor unhealthy characteristic, but represents an essence quality in me that must be reflected in the interests of my significant other.

How then do we determine whether a particular quality in a potential candidate is an occasional foible or is severe enough to operate as a disqualifier? How do we know if the absence of something, such as supporting the arts, becomes a disqualifier? We will get to that point in the next section. For now, I want you to turn to the end of the chapter and start working on your list. What are the things that you know you would not be able to stand or be without in a relationship?

℞ ALTERING YOUR LIST

Now that you have started your list, you have a relatively decent first line of defense in place; however, as you gain experience from using it and as you consider the accurateness of the disqualifiers, keep in mind that this list is not static. In other words, you may alter your list as you work with the other aspects of relationships later in the book, specifically matching essence qualities and identifying those things that, while they are not disqualifiers, they certainly can cause problems. Your list may also change as you experience a break-up, or as you clarify and understand your own essences. When I first began dating in college, I had never heard of essence qualities and did not understand the level of importance that high goal-driven behavior played in my own life. Consequently, it wasn't something I noticed the presence or absence of in another as I considered potential partners. This seems strange looking back, because at that time I was competing at the international level in athletics. It was only in recent years, using this model while dating my husband, Darren, that I added "lack of excellence orientation" to my disqualifier list. We will examine this idea more in the essence-matching chapter.

Women in my workshops who are grappling with whether something they have encountered really needs to be a disqualifier or not will ask me: if you want it badly enough, is it possible to overcome the difficulties presented by a disqualifier? Certainly! I say to them. I remind them of the shoe and the university example. You can cut the ends off the shoes that don't fit and let your toes stick out or attend the desired university but major in a different subject. "Yes," you say, "but such changes are either ridiculous or produce fundamental change." Good observation, and therein lies the purpose and function of knowing your what your disqualifiers are. If you can imagine situations when a disqualifier might work, it might be better classed as a red flag, which I cover in chapter 11 on "Red Flags." While the toeless shoes would probably be considered as an unacceptable solution, the shift of academic major may not. In the final analysis the items on your list should therefore either be something which would destroy any relationship or which the cost to overcome it is just too high.

Developing the Right Mindset

℞

Remember the purpose of this chapter is to not only guide you in the creation of a list of disqualifiers, but also to help you get into the right mindset to use them. It saddens me greatly to think of all the bad marriages that are made because one person was willing to compromise too much to overlook something that they really couldn't stand or of which they were afraid. The application of disqualifiers often takes great courage. I'll never forget a young woman whom I once counseled that eventually showed great courage. She became pregnant early in a dating relationship. An additional complication was that she was unsure who the father was since she had been intimate with two young men. By the time she knew that she was pregnant, she was regularly dating one of them, John. As the story continued to unfolded, John often revealed extreme anger by breaking chairs and punching holes in walls. She forgave this as "her fault" initially but became concerned when he continued over a series of months to display his anger physically. He wasn't hitting her— yet. She eventually chose to be a single mother, as she realized that she could not live with this threatening disqualifier.

Other times, we don't want to really see the disqualifier because we're so "in love" that we have our proverbial "rose-colored glasses" on or because there's an extenuating circumstance that creates emotion, like the pregnancy in the above story. The ability of strong emotions to lure us off our chosen path is so remarkable that we will spend the next chapter helping you recognize the ones to which you are most susceptible.

For now, just know that the right mindset includes not only exhibiting courage, but also the ability to overcoming our natural tendency to be accepting. We've spent the last one hundred years embracing diversity and operate in a culture that is based on acceptance. To say: "I'm not going to date you because I don't like this one thing," goes against that learned attitude. In the business world recognizing when to and actually taking the steps to fire someone is an uncomfortable but important component of a successful organization. Apply the same fortitude in relationships so that you maintain your emotional health.

USING YOUR LIST OF DISQUALIFIERS

Using your list is a little more daunting though, than just changing it. I started the chapter wishing that we had a crystal ball. But we don't, and we are, unfortunately, more willing to use blinders than not, even when we know the devastation that disqualifiers can wreak in a relationship. I again say to you: if you find the presence of just one, you should end the relationship. Since I understand that this is so much easier said than done, let me give you another analogy: imagine that you are about to fly across the country in order to spend Thanksgiving with your family. Most of us have watched the pre-flight check process that is involved in confirming a plane's readiness for safe travel. In my example, you are the passenger; the plane is a potential "Mr. Right" and the plane's components are all of the qualities that make up this particular guy. In our scenario, there are four different points in time that you might find a mechanical problem and take action.

Ideal: As you arrive at the airport and approach your gate, you hear that the plane that was originally scheduled for the trip had developed a mechanical problem. Not only did the airline find the issue early, they have replaced the plane and your flight will still be on time. Result: there was a problem, you recognized it and did not date the guy; you moved on and are talking to the next person.

Irritating: You have boarded the plane, but it's grounded due to a mechanical difficulty. They have you get off the plane, and after a two-hour delay, you're re-scheduled on a later flight. Result: you dated the guy a couple of times but saw issues of concern, now you're flustered and upset but you move on to the next individual and eventually get to your destination.

Compromised: You have already boarded the plane, and it's on the tarmac making its way to the runway. You're excited about your visit and the thrill of take off. As you reach cruising altitude, someone notices a fuel leak out of one of the engines (this happened to my friend while flying with my children) and you circle back, wait to burn enough fuel and come in on an emergency approach but land safely. Result: while you have became emotionally involved, and really hoped he was the right one, you applied your disqualifier and landed the plane, effectively ending the relationship. You're safe but distraught and you might need to wait for some healing to occur before you enter into the next relationship.

Destructive: You're in the air, there's a mechanical problem that got missed *or* ignored, it breaks and the engine self-destructs. The pilots manage a screaming emergency landing, injuring several passengers. Result: You marry the guy, and either was blinded by love to the disqualifier or ignored it and during marriage find that the disqualifier could not be overcome, and while you landed in one piece, the horror and pain of the process leaves damage to all parties.

The moral of the story is to apply disqualifiers as soon as possible. As uncomfortable as it may seem, early application is less painful to you than waiting or ignoring them.

Given the stunning complexity and subtle nuance of human behavior, now we consider a thorny problem: all of the items on the psychologist's list and most of the items on the personally-determined list don't operate in a simple world of black and white. In fact, only a few are clear-cut: a person either smokes or he doesn't; he either is or is not a member of your religious denomination; a person either is or is not addicted to substances. But the majority of items operate on some sort of continuous scale. If a person ranks low on the scale for a particular item does this serve as a disqualifier? How about if someone used to possess certain negative qualities and now only vestiges remain? Consequently, when you are dating, identification of disqualifiers in another person is sometimes easy, at other times more challenging. How can we know? Here are four suggestions I consistently use in counseling to assist you:

Some things are fairly easily determined early in the relationship. These can be seen by just observing the person in interactions with others, by interacting with him in a casual setting, or on a first date. It is easy to observe if a person smokes, drinks, swears, is negative or hostile or has a bitter spirit. Sometimes we're lucky, and the guy will pick a fight on the first date, or tell you that he doesn't like professional women. That's a no-brainer. You can end the date with a "thank you," and move on from there. This initial encounter may be sufficient to discontinue your interest in a particular relationship.

People are typically on their best behavior early in a relationship, but as the interactions continue, hidden things begin to emerge. Even so, personality traits and temperament issues that you consider disqualifiers may be buried several dates into the process. If you have your list in place you will be more sensitized to potential problems and are likely to be aware of them as they emerge. Disqualifiers associated with personal qualities are more likely to show up later in the relationship such as abusive behavior, selfishness, rigidity, a controlling nature or dishonesty. In your list you might not like a person who punches walls when he's angry, but you don't know that this wonderful man you're dating does that until six months into the relationship. The caution here is that by this time, it's likely that you already have some level of emotional involvement, and rather than stay in the relationship and justify it with the compromise mentality, you must have the courage to end it.

Consult with others who know the person well. Through this mechanism, insights about certain qualities may emerge that you didn't discover earlier. While it is true that one person's report may be erroneous, remember what we presented earlier where we considered "similar themes from independent sources." This was a particularly difficult step for me as I dated Darren long distance. He gave me permission to talk with people that had counseled him, friends and even his brother's ex-wife. And while I didn't discover any disqualifiers, if several objective, reliable people had independently identified a similar problem, I was prepared to break off the relationship. If through talking to these sources you uncovered useful information, you would do well to take notice.

Testing. Many counseling practices use some form of testing. The point here is, the earlier the better. Also if you feel generalized discomfort in the relationship but can't put your finger on what is wrong, testing may help. The MBTI (Meyers-Briggs Type Indicator) [20] the 16PF (16 Personality Factor Questionnaire) [21] the TJTA (Taylor-Johnson Temperament Analysis) [22] and a variety of others provide insights into behaviors and attitudes that are not so easily observed. Find out where testing is available and then both of you go and get tested. You can then have fun comparing the results. Of course, if serious problems emerge, then it won't be so fun. But isn't brief discomfort worth taking the time to ensure that you marry someone without disqualifiers?

A Note to Those in a Relationship

℞

If you are reading this chapter and are already in a relationship, go back and consider what your disqualifiers should have been (or would be in a future relationship). Remember that it is possible to love so intensely, desire so greatly, hope so desperately that a particular relationship can work out, that you ignore the simple realities presented in this chapter. You may find yourself hoping beyond hope that the one disqualifier that he has will change over time. I just counseled a younger couple through this process and it was very enlightening for them. While they were very much "in love," deeply attracted to one another, the one is a concertmaster of an orchestra, the other a cowboy. The concertmaster knew that she needed to live in a city that had an orchestra. The cowboy, of course, wants a cattle ranch in the middle of nowhere. The musician considers her home her quiet haven away from the world. The cowboy wants his house bursting with people, all the time. They broke off their relationship, and while they are still dealing with the emotional complexities of being around one another in daily life and being attracted to each other, the whole process has been made much easier—and I suspect a lot less painful—because they made their decision based on reason instead of emotion. So I'm going to say it again. Even if you are intensely in love with him, break off the relationship as long as that disqualifier is present.

The challenge of course is halting the progression of the relationship once you have identified a disqualifier. Going back to the HR model with which I started this section on "take a look outward," the hardest thing to do in HR is to fire someone because we know the repercussions; we don't like to tell someone they're unworthy or they failed to measure up. A relationship has the same complexity and emotional barriers because when you break off a relationship with someone, you are essentially firing them from your potential organization called a family.

A Final Word

As you compile your list of behaviors, know that this is a difficult subject because no matter how strongly I warn you, it is tough to implement this list. In a way, it's like all those resolutions and commitments you've made over the years, like "I'm going to lose weight" or "spend less time watching TV and more time reading." Any decision to change behavior requires a firm commitment from you. And make no mistake, by suggesting that you compile this list and urging you to follow it, I'm helping you to change your past patterns of how you assessed potential mates. It is likely that in your past, you've either applied the wrong criteria to decisions about your partners or you didn't hold to the decision that you made using the criteria you set. In the next chapter we will examine things that will attempt to pull you off course, to blind you to your resolve.

Finally, I want to make something very clear here, as I end this chapter. There are disqualifiers and then there are essence-quality challenges. You may have a successful marriage despite some essence-quality challenges. You may form a successful relationship despite some blind spots; you may even have an outstanding marriage in which you never wrote down the qualities of your ideal partner. But the buck stops here. If you marry someone with disqualifiers, you essentially guarantee failure, or at best, a severely challenged relationship. I want you to have tools to lessen the risk, fear, and frustration that can accompany the process of finding the right life partner. I want to make the process a little more objective for you, and if that sounds harsh, so be it. Remember, I warned you there's no romance in this chapter, only the cold, hard fact of truth—the truth about your disqualifiers.

List of Personal Disqualifiers

Name: _____ Date: _____

Disqualifiers from research findings:

Put a check by any that you think may be present

☐ Hostility
☐ Bitterness
☐ Selfishness
☐ Rigid/uncompromising
☐ Tactless
☐ Egotistical
☐ Controlling
☐ Dishonest
☐ Cruel
☐ Poor communication skills

☐ Manipulative
☐ Reactive thinker
☐ Emotionally unstable
☐ Overly sensitive
☐ Excessive dependency
☐ Severe psychological disorders
☐ Uncontrolled anger
☐ Habitually critical
☐ Obsessive or compulsive behavior

Your Personally Determined Disqualifiers:

1. _____

2. _____

3. _____

4. _____

5. _____

6. _____

7. _____

8. _____

9. _____

10. _____

Chapter 9

LURE OF THE SIRENS

Biasers: The Terrifying Power
to Distort or Blind

D isqualifiers, while they may be distasteful to identify and emotionally difficult to use, aren't actually the hardest things to confront in the process of "taking a look outward." If we go back to our Human Resource model, you've now identified what you want and don't want, but the next step is to learn to recognize things that will give you a false impression or distort your ability to read the potential candidate accurately and determine a good fit. You need to take a look at those things that can get in the way of you making a good decision.

To help you understand what I'm talking about, let me tell you a story. It's taken from Greek mythology, and it's about creatures called the Sirens. For those of you who know the story, you'll quickly know the connection I'm trying to make. The Sirens in the myth were seductive creatures with the head of a female and the body of a bird. They lived on an island that Odysseus, the hero from the epic poem, *The Odyssey*[1] (attributed to the Greek poet, Homer) had to pass in order to get home. The Sirens were known for beautiful singing that was both irresistible and enchanting. It was incredibly sweet and seductive, but it was also deadly. The sirens sang the song to lure mariners to their destruction on the rocks surrounding the Siren's island. Odysseus had been warned about this, but wanted to hear the joy of the song anyway, so he ordered his sailors to stop their ears with wax and then tie him to the mast of the ship. He instructed them not to release him, no matter how hard he begged. When he actually heard the song, not only was the melody everything that he had hoped to hear, but he found that the words of the song were even more enticing. They promised him everything that he wanted: ripe wisdom and immortality. Odysseus longed to follow the song and all that it promised him, but the crew followed his instructions refusing to release him, and they rowed past the Siren's island without harm.

That is what this next chapter is all about: those things that promise you everything that you've ever wanted in a relationship—emotional closeness, an end to loneliness—but are the very things that can bash your successful relationships on the rocks of disaster unless you take the right precautions against them.

In our seminars, Darren and I have created a word that is roughly equivalent to the Sirens' lure, those things that distort your ability to see clearly and thus (like the Sirens) pull you away from your primary goal. We call them "biasers." It comes from the word "bias" which means the unfair preference for or dislike of something or distortion of results. We all experience biasers in a variety of ways and circumstances. In the context of this book the goal you seek is an excellent marriage. Thus biasers are factors that detract you from reaching your goal of an excellent marriage. Just like the Sirens, biasers can be so powerful, so deceiving, so sweet that they are very difficult to resist. Many give in. In fact we often *want* to give in if it will only *stop* the loneliness and need for companionship, the promise of something beyond the void one is living in. The result contributes to the mess we see today of 50 percent divorce rate and 80 percent unhappy rate in North American marriages. It reminds me of a comment from the 1974 movie *Alice Doesn't Live Here Anymore*. Alice (played by Ellen Burstyn) following a devastating divorce is asked, "Why did you marry him?" Her response: "Because he was a great kisser." [2] In this case the siren call of "great kissing" blinded Alice to the impending disaster: an impossible marriage and a painful divorce.

This chapter, then, is asking you to become aware of your biasers and be warned against their lure. Not only do I want you to know what they are and how they can pull you off course, but I want you to recognize the need for friends and activities that will tie you to the mast, as it were, so that you can sail past the temptations safely and reach your intended destination.

THE TWO TYPES OF BIASERS EXPLORED

There are two different forces that cause biases in our ability to make accurate decisions or stay on the planned course:

- Intense emotions, and
- Erroneous information or perceptions.

Intense emotions are the Sirens' call to intimacy, warmth, nurturance, safety. But the Sirens lie, as do our emotions. Erroneous information (such as the fairy-tale marriage) and erroneous perceptions (for instance, that anyone who can kiss *that* well has got to be a good marriage prospect) lead many to their doom. This chapter equips you to guard against both types of biasers. Although we can identify these two forces separately, they are closely linked because strong emotions often trigger the inaccurate perceptions.

Errors of Judgment Due to Strong Emotions

One of the most foundational psychological principles explains the relationship between clear thinking and strong emotions. It has been found that as emotions increase, the ability to think clearly diminishes. When emotions are extreme, clear thought for most people largely disappears. Back in chapter 4, we looked at the emotional germs from past relationships that can infect your future. These are the strong emotions that you must handle before you can move on into any healthy relationship. In that chapter, we talked about strong emotions that come from the baggage of broken relationships and whose very presence determines whether or not you should be dating. Once health was restored, I guided you through self-assessment and identification of your essence qualities. Now you have an image of your ideal partner in mind; in fact you may have met someone and are trying to apply these principles and guidelines. In this chapter I bring back into the forefront the idea of strong emotions because regardless of the type—positive or negative—intense emotions will lure us off course. If someone is overwhelmed with joy, anticipation, and excitement, sound judgment flees and an array of "gullible" mistakes follow: a purchase that sends them into bankruptcy, a business choice that fills their garage with worthless products, acceptance of a marriage proposal that condemns them to fifty years of quiet desperation. When a person is overcome by negative emotions, such as anger, fear or hostility, an array of self- or other-destructive behaviors frequently occur. When emotions are aroused to fever pitch in a sexual context, STDs, AIDS, unwanted pregnancy, or shame and feelings of guilt are the frequent results. These types of emotions can continue to be biasers; however, in this chapter we examine how *all* emotionally healthy people are biased both mentally and physically with intense feelings arising from many sources as they move forward in seeking lasting relationships.

℞ *Errors of Judgment Due to Flawed Perceptions or Information*

We get our information about what makes a good marriage from all kinds of places, not to mention our earlier conditioning from the fairy-tale model. Our friend tells us one thing, that talk show host tells us another. Much of the information we hear and read influences our thinking. Not being experts, we accumulate unedited tidbits from here and there and compile them into our knowledge base. Some examples follow:

Sometimes we determine our choices based on the opinions of friends. A classic example: one divorced woman talks with another divorced woman about what makes for a successful marriage. Is it possible that valid information could emerge from such a discussion? Maybe, but which details are valid and which are dangerously flawed? I would be loath to consult eight-times-married (and divorced) Elizabeth Taylor for principles of marital success. Jesus said it straight: "If the blind lead the blind, they both fall into the ditch."

A good story is another way of acquiring erroneous information. One of my students relates that her parents married within three weeks of first meeting, and they continue to enjoy an excellent marriage. The story is true but is dreadfully misleading. As I have pointed out before, objective analysis of individuals who meet and marry within thirty days finds an almost complete failure rate.[3] So while in that one instance a happy marriage resulted, it is not the norm and therefore not a model we should follow.

Another challenge is that people use the wrong information in their observations. They see an apparently happily married couple that has obvious personality mismatches or that come from dramatically different backgrounds. The naïve observer may assume that these differences are the cause of their marital success. The reality? If their relationship *is* successful, it is probably despite the mismatches and the background differences, not because of them. Not only that, but the "happy" marital interactions visible to the casual observer may be a façade that covers difficulties that occur within the privacy of their home.

Then there is the issue of misattribution. Misattribution is coming up with the *wrong* reason for a particular outcome. For instance, let's say that you divorce and someone asks why. If in your response you list a rich array of faults of your former spouse but don't believe you contributed to the problem, it is almost certain there are serious holes in your understanding. Such erroneous judgment is likely to ensure continued difficulties in your relational life.

℞

At the end of this chapter we consider the fairly extensive case of Walter and Amy (not their real names) who experienced, many times over, both types of biasers on their way to an impossible marriage. But before we begin their story, I'd like to draw an analogy to help you get a grip on the strength and urgency of biasers *and* what they can do to your sound judgment. It has nothing to do with romantic relationships but it is something I bet that most of you can relate to. It had to do with a trip I was making with my twins.

They were seven-years-old at the time, and we, the three of us, were driving twenty-seven hundred miles in four days from Alberta to Alabama to visit my mother. We were two days into the trip and more or less on schedule when we began to pick up signs about a roadside water/theme park. The girls went off (just like Sirens) squealing with excitement and pleas to stop and have some fun. Well, I rationalized—my first mistake. We had been driving for two days and weren't that many hours from our reserved hotel room. It was hot, the girls were cramped in the car, and I had road fatigue…and well, we took the exit and pulled into the parking lot. My first sense of dismay came when the attendant asked for thirty dollars per person for entry. And that was just the beginning of tribulation. We spent money on outrageously priced food, on the t-shirts they just *had* to have, even the glow-in-the-dark thingies. The girls squealed in delight as they initially got drenched in the water area, but then argued and cried the rest of the time due to travel fatigue and overexcitement. A couple of hours later, as we got back on the Interstate, the girls were crying. They were wet and cold, the hotel was hours away, and I was worn out. And to top it all off, just when I had finally drifted off to sleep in the hotel, one of the girls sat up and literally exploded from a tummy upset. So which was worse: listening to and resisting their pleas for a side trip to an exciting park or living with the results from giving in to an impulsive decision? Read on, and I'll provide an answer at the end of the chapter as I guide you to a path of clear thinking.

℞ RELATIONAL AREAS WHERE BIASES ARE MOST LIKELY TO OCCUR

What follows are five areas in which biases are particularly lethal: 1) the need for closeness, 2) loneliness, 3) physical attractiveness, 4) fear that no one is there for you, and 5) sexual urgency. These topics, while not comprehensive, should assist you in making application to other areas. Before we get started, keep in mind that gender impacts the strength and which types of biasers are most likely to be experienced. For instance, a study, conducted by my husband while at UCLA, explored how men and women differ in their attraction to each other. Two factors were considered: 1) physical attractiveness, and 2) the altruism and generosity of each subject. Participants were asked how important these two factors are in three different hypothetical situations: 1) a single date; 2) exclusive dating; and 3) marriage. The results of this study are consistent with many others: in all three situations the personal qualities of the individual were more important to women than to men. And in all three situations, beauty was more important to the men than it was to the women. Although the findings did show that in the marriage situation, even men begin considering personal qualities as increasingly important.

As you read the following examples of biasers, try to determine how susceptible you are to each, as well as think of others that have not been listed here. If I had been writing this book for the men, we would probably consider physical attractiveness or beauty as the leading biaser. As it is, I'll begin by cautioning you to be wary of your need for closeness.

Desire for Nurturing Closeness

Many who have just experienced divorce or a broken relationship indicate that it is not the absence of sex they miss as much as the lack of closeness. Even sleeping next to someone can be an ultimately nourishing and satisfying experience, but when your partner is no longer there, that closeness is gone, and you long for it.

It all comes down to the power of touch. In 1941 famed psychologist, René Spits, heard of an orphanage in his own city with a greater than 40 percent mortality rate of infants. When he explored the situation he found everything in order: the facility was sanitary, the meals were appropriate and nutritious, the staff was adequately trained. The only difficulty was that there were twelve infants for every caregiver. The children were literally dying from lack of physical contact.[4] A number of other studies have documented the importance of touch and closeness in infancy and early childhood. While the importance of adult touching has not been nearly so thoroughly documented, it stands to reason that if little bodies need touch then big bodies do too. Remember what my husband found in the study of 229 divorced individuals, that non-sexual touch was second only to a rich support network in the recovery process.

So, desiring some form of human touch is natural. But, what you must be watchful of is if you're making wrong decisions because this need has become overwhelming. If you are craving human touch, that's fine. Just don't get into a relationship because you're desire for touch is so strong that you'll hook up with anyone. Find ways to satisfy that desire before you embark on a serious relationship. Take a dance class, get a pet, hug your friends more, join a church singles group, even volunteer at a nursing home. Old people crave touch as much as anyone else! I remember seeing a documentary about elderly people who were recruited to lightly caress premature infants. The study found that the premature baby gained weight faster and the elderly person became happier and healthier. Not surprising. Seek activities and associations where touch is provided generously. Beware, however, if touch moves in the romantic or sexual direction.

Loneliness

Close kin, of course, to a desire for physical closeness is emotional closeness. When we don't have it, it's called loneliness. It is not a small problem. Research suggests that 25 percent of people in North America suffer chronically and severely from loneliness.[5] I suspect that many of you reading this book experience some degree of loneliness because you've either just experienced a break up or you haven't been in a relationship for a long time. It's not a pleasant feeling, and when it becomes overwhelming, you tend to make stupid mistakes. One of my clients recalls a story of when she was a graduate student in New York. She was suffering from severe chronic fatigue, extremely sensitive to smoke and perfume, and so she was unable to socialize much. She was intensely lonely.

About two months before she was to move out of New York, she had an encounter with a waiter in a restaurant she frequented. She had been flirting with him for months. One day, she was walking by the restaurant, and he happened to be leaning against the door jam. She stopped to talk to him, and after a few pleasantries, he looked deep into her eyes and said "I want to make love to you." She didn't even know his name, but he seemed decent enough. He was a dancer so he was gorgeous, and he had the most soulful eyes. She invited him over that night, and the next two months became an emotional roller coaster. He would see her and then not return her calls. The night before she was to leave the city for good, he was supposed to come over and spend the night as a final good-bye. He never called, and she never heard from him again. Because of her compromised state of health, she had a difficult time recovering emotionally from that episode. In our session, after we had covered the problems that occur with intense emotional loneliness, she recognized that she acted very foolishly and she could have saved herself untold emotional grief if she had found a less volatile outlet for her loneliness.

℞ Social psychology actually identifies two types of loneliness that people deal with: *social loneliness* and *emotional loneliness*.[6] Social loneliness is associated with lack of a number of enjoyable friendship-type relationships. An individual in an otherwise happy marriage may suffer from social loneliness if the life is devoid of a rich network of friends. Emotional loneliness, by contrast, is typically associated with lack of an intimate partner.

Emotional loneliness is the much more daunting problem that we've been discussing. It represents a large portion of the powerful biological urges that attract the sexes. It represents needs that are so deep that they at times defy description. I'm sure I have encountered hundreds of people who have suffered severely because they would like to be married but various circumstances have denied it happening. Perhaps they are shy and find it difficult to initiate contact with persons of the opposite sex. Perhaps they feel that they are not attractive enough or not sexy enough to attract another. Perhaps situational constraints (such as living in a small community where there are no available others) prohibit meaningful romantic opportunities. Perhaps personal constraints such as a demanding job, needy parents, or financial challenges simply don't allow for that type of pursuit. Whatever the cause, for many the frequent comment is: "During the week when I'm working, things are okay, but on the weekends and in particular, Friday night, I hit bottom." If you find that your emotional loneliness is causing you to make bad decisions, explore ways to enhance your social network. Psychology finds that a "confidant" relationship, a really close friend with whom you can share anything, can fulfill this need to some extent. When you have a large number of friends, a confidant relationship is more likely to emerge.

* * * * *

These first two biasers focused on absence of fulfilled needs and they make sense if you step back and think about it: I long for touch and I long for companionship. The next lure though, is one of the big visual enticements, the one that we may think we're not tempted by because we're strong, independent women who know better.

Physical Attractiveness   ℞

Ah yes! A thousand magazines celebrate it, constructions workers ogle at it, acting agencies drool over it, movies eulogize it, and most people, it seems, enjoy it. The problem is that physical attractiveness is not a very good predictor of marital success. Beauty has been made legend by poets and writers, but scientific research reveals some simple realities concerning beauty. The reality includes some positives: those who are beautiful are more likely to be socially skilled than their less fetching peers. The beautiful are found to have about the same level of overall life-satisfaction as less attractive people suggesting that the advantages of beauty are balanced out by some disadvantages. But most startling is beautiful people are significantly less likely than others to have successful marriages.

Beauty operates as a biaser for most people because of the "halo   ℞
effect." The halo effect causes people to assume that just because there is one salient positive trait (in this case beauty) that there is an array of other equally positive qualities such as warmth, passion, intelligence, desire, sexual urgency and many others.[7] But, as Huckleberry Finn might put it, "It just ain't so." External beauty may cover all the foibles shared

by the less attractive: anger, hostility, bitterness, a critical spirit, egotism, stupidity, coldness.

We live in a society that obsesses about beauty. The insidious effect of this conditioning is very difficult to counteract. It doesn't matter whether or not we wish to embrace those values; they are absorbed while we are still young children. We notice that good-looking babies get more attention, many high schools have beauty queens, magazines feature the most physically perfect, and the dazzling beauty-contest winners can achieve national attention. It makes not the slightest difference whether or not we *are* those beautiful people; we will absorb the attitudes of our parents and those around us and internalized the prevailing attitude that beauty is "king" (or queen). It is difficult to escape the clutches of this absorbed viewpoint.

It is important in a marriage that you find your partner personally appealing. Appreciate, however, that external beauty is only one of an array of characteristics that should be considered. Beauty of spirit and character is even more important. Think with your mind and realize that physical beauty will fade over time but many of the personal qualities will not only remain but will continue to develop. Realize that beauty has a powerful tendency to bias or to distort one's perception of other realities. Fight those tendencies. Enjoy beauty, but consider the more important qualities associated with marital success when you make a choice as important as selecting a life partner.

And finally ladies, remember the results from the UCLA study referenced at the beginning of this section. In each situation ranging from a single date, to exclusive dating, to marriage, physical attractiveness was more important to the men than it was to the women. How should you apply this? Seek men who don't conform to the norm, who place greater emphasis on personal qualities than on beauty. Keep in mind therefore, that as women we are going to place greater weight on the attractiveness of personal qualities and will likely be the one that brings up such topics for conversation and comparison.

* * * * *

Okay, now that I've given you the obvious, let's pinpoint those biasers that lurk around us all. If you ever have thought, "*sigh*, I've been looking and searching for months or maybe even years for a life mate, someone interested in the things I'm interested in, someone who values personal qualities, someone who…" In other words, you've been looking, and looking, and looking, and the longevity of search itself gives rise for us to consider the next bias.

Fear That There's No One There   ℞

The desire to be "in a relationship" seems to be a universal human experience. Statistics show that in North America, 95 percent have been legally married at least once by age fifty.[8] And when you are not in a relationship, whether that is a recent occurrence or a long-term situation, oftentimes, you fear that you're never going to be in another relationship again. Fear is a slippery emotion because so often it is unfounded. Studies show that a good deal of fear and anxiety is quite pointless. In the average person, of the events or things that cue fear or anxiety:

- 40 percent never happen
- 30 percent are in your past and thus cannot be changed
- 12 percent are needless
- 10 percent are small and petty
- 8 percent are real (and some of those you have no control over)[9]

Fear, however, can be a powerful force to motivate bad decisions about relationships. Conversely it can paralyze you from making decisions. When we break up, we may think: I'm afraid that I won't find another man because I'm not thin enough. Or, perhaps, you're shy and you fear that this will keep you from finding a life partner. Or, perhaps you live in a place where the pickin's are thin, so to speak, and so you fear that your very location will keep you from finding the right someone who is both compatible and potentially interested in you.

Whatever your fear, it is wise to remember Franklin Roosevelt's famous phrase from his first inaugural address in 1933. It was during the depths of the depression, and to rally the morale of the nation, he gave us these immortal words: "The only thing we have to fear is fear itself." The statement implies that fear itself is of such a paralyzing nature that if we defeat fear, we will then have the courage and energy to effectively attack any other problem. This is a valid perspective when it comes to seeking for a potential marriage partner. If you can overcome your fear of being lonely, then you can begin the process of finding the right life partner.

The reality is that if you feel that you are unmarriageable due to controllable causes, the time will eventually come to make a choice (undoubtedly several choices): will I continue unmarried because I possess these qualities, or, even worse, will I get into a relationship that eventually terminates because of these challenges *or* will I have the courage to confront and change the things that need to be confronted and changed? (Think back to the end of chapter 5 on "The Straight Truth about Self" and handling the negative personal qualities.) If the choice is for change, I congratulate you. Like the Subway guy who lost over two hundred pounds because he knew that he needed to confront his weight problem, confronting your fears may be painful at first, but once you do, you can have a completely different—and healthy—life stretching ahead. The choice before you is: will I live in misery and isolation for a lifetime or will I make the courageous choices to confront my fear and make the changes that I feel may alter the outcome and give me more confidence?

But what if you feel you are highly marriageable and you are still waiting? The question is straightforward but the answer is difficult to live with: will I succumb to the fear and marry someone not well suited and live in misery and isolation or will I make the courageous choice to remain single? Hard facts, hard choices, and if you are confronted by this bias I encourage you to have fortitude to stay the course, and keep looking for the right guy. Beware, however, that waiting will likely yield additional urgencies.

℞ *Sexual Urgency*

Part of the "chemistry" that happens when we meet someone is often sexual. And it is usually intense. You're attracted to someone; he comes up behind you and lightly runs his finger under the strap of your dress. He's fixing it because it's twisted, but *whew*. You feel electric currents run through you; you literally become weak in the knees. That's a healthy response. Because our bodies are programmed to reproduce, we, of course, are going to respond to sexy stimuli.

With this we encounter a biaser even more powerful than beauty. Here is the entire spectrum of sexual touch, from the slightest brush (quite capable of creating a powerful reaction if the touch comes from the right person) to full sexual intimacy. Unfortunately, the power of touch is so great that there are millions who would rather be in an impossible relationship and cling to the warmth of an embrace than to be without it and hope for something better. The fatal flaw is that in those poor or impossible relationships, the intimacies eventually become cold or cease entirely.

Taking a simple clinical look at sexual desire we discover that it is an instinctual hunger that is aroused by external stimuli, internal emotions and physiological need. Disregarding opinions on the appropriateness of sexual activity prior to marriage for purposes of this book, I focus only on the astonishing ability of sexual touch to create strong emotions and block your ability to make sound choices, for both you *and* your partner. Reducing sexual tension can be as simple as avoiding situations, reading material, and movies that stimulate desire and remind you of what you are missing. Instead choose non-sexual activities and interests that you can enjoy, either as an individual or in groups, without the pressure of intimacy. I do sympathize though as I type this. Its one thing to talk about sexual guidelines and restraint from within a fulfilling marriage; it's another thing to be where you are as you read this. I can hear the humor in Darren's voice as he speaks frankly about sexual issues to our disconcerted college groups and points out that when you're young and single you probably think about sex a large percent of the time, but once you're married even the most enthusiastic sex-life will take up only about two percent of your marriage experience. That leaves a whopping ninety-eight percent of your time to fill together, further emphasizing the importance of shared compatibilities.

The closeness and sense of commitment that arises from sexual intimacy creates such powerful biases that it is almost impossible to see past it to rationally assess whether the two of you are martially compatible.

* * * * *

There are many biasers and sirens that research identifies as potentially threatening to your decision-making process. In the story that follows, you will recognize some that we have already discussed as well as new ones. While there are biasers that systematically affect all of us, there may be some that are particularly challenging to you. Try to identify, as you read this true story, which of these would have sidetracked you as well (or to put it more bluntly, slammed you upside the head and knocked you out of all your rational senses).

THE STORY OF WALTER AND AMY

Walter was a sociology graduate student at a leading university when the story takes place. Walter had been through a divorce a couple years earlier, felt that he was not in a good setting for meeting available others, was not particularly skilled socially anyway, and felt eager to be in a relationship that would lead to marriage. While such desires sound normal enough, Walter's desire to be in relationship was intense. He was sick to death of being single, lonely, and, being a proactive person, wanted to do something about it. Enter bias number one:

An intense need to be in a relationship: There is nothing wrong with either the need or the desire, but when the need is excessive, many blunders typically follow. He discovered dating services that showed pictures and had brief descriptions of Asian women eager to marry an American. Walter would leaf through the various magazines from several of the agencies, look at the pictures, read the descriptions and grow increasingly excited about the possibilities of obtaining the warmth of a life partner (without the effort of dating) by making contacts with these women. Several of the women responded to Walter's letters, and it was evident that there was both eagerness and willingness on the part of those who responded. Excitement grew as Walter began the sorting procedure. Since marriage was not possible without actually flying over to Asia and meeting the individual in person, the idea of actually dating several of them was not an option. The situation, in Walter's mind, required narrowing down to one person before the very expensive trip took place. Here we encounter bias number two.

Choices are made in the absence of thorough knowledge: Because of the high cost of contact in this setting, there was no valid opportunity (Walter felt) to actually meet other women. Bias number three quickly emerged. Walter chose one woman. We'll call her Amy. When a tentative choice had been made and interaction accelerated (mostly letters and phone calls) powerful images of the perfect wife emerged and nights were spent dreaming of pleasures that might soon become reality.

Intense love for an unsubstantiated image: In short, the intense emotional arousal blinded Walter to the potential pitfalls. It failed to register with him that his love object, Amy, might possess serious flaws or that impossible differences might exist between them. The letters were now augmented with frequent phone calls. The letters dripped with unbridled affection; the calls spoke of some substantive matters but shimmering infatuation predominated most conversations. The fourth bias then emerged:

Belief in the accuracy of an image without actual contact: Walter and Amy essentially became engaged by phone and mail without ever seeing each other. Walter thought that from letters, phone calls, and descriptions that a clear image was emerging. And, he was right. A clear image was emerging, but it was unrelated to the reality of the person who controlled his affections. The fifth bias immediately followed.

No consultation with objective others: Most of these contacts were made without the knowledge of any of Walter's friends or family. Only as the relationship began to move solidly toward the engagement stage did Walter begin to talk with others. The choice of engagement took place outside of the advice or knowledge of anyone else. Once the choice to become engaged had been made, several thousands of dollars were set aside for the trip over and several weeks in Hong Kong. Bias number six now moved into position:

Inoculation against any advice due to the certainty of choice: Once the trip and the engagement were in place (Walter never told others that they were already engaged; he realized that such a choice in the absence of contact was sure to arouse negative responses), Walter began to inform family and friends of the impending trip. Even though the "E" word (engagement) was not ever used, the simple reality was that Walter's interactions with family and friends were designed to deceive, so along comes bias number seven:

Deception of others: As Walter began to divulge even his sanitized version of the story people quickly anticipated the real purpose and set up a shrill series of protests about the scheduled trip. Walter was so blinded he was unwilling to hear any of it. He had already discovered the "truth" (he was convinced that the choice of engagement was correct) and was able to ward off any criticism. We dub this attitude "the engaged person's disease." When one's mind is made up, when that person is truly inoculated, no information or argument can shift his or her perspective. The overtures of friends and family were summarily dismissed—a serious error indeed. Specifically, Walter's brother pleaded with Walter to call off the trip but to no avail. Additional evidence emerged shortly before the trip was to be made. It turned out that Amy was technically married. She was from the Philippines where (according to her story) there is no legal form of divorce. If you are rich enough, you can bribe a judge and he will take the documents out of your file. In Amy's case she had no children and had had no contact with her former husband for over three years (he had abandoned her). Bias number eight now emerges:

Self-deception: Walter convinced himself that her long-since defunct marriage was no problem despite the fact that a divorce had not occurred. The final bias emerged only after the trip to Hong Kong, their point of meeting.

A feeling of entrapment: Walter flew to Hong Kong. At the airport he met Amy for the first time. He found her smaller and less attractive than her pictures indicated. He remembered quickly an additional reality; people provide only pictures that make them look better than they really do. If Walter had met Amy on the street, he would have never had the slightest attraction but now he felt trapped and obligated. He had chosen engagement in good faith and now he felt they must go through with the marriage. A few days later they did. Amy and Walter were together about five weeks during the Hong Kong venture and spent another two weeks (in the Philippines) three months later during the Christmas season. Walter found her to be honest in her desire to please and commit to the relationship, but Walter and Amy were as mismatched as any two people could possibly be: Walter had a Ph.D.; Amy it turned out was below average IQ. He took Amy with him to visit professors in several of the local universities; Amy couldn't begin to understand the conversation. Amy said that she had a college degree and apparently did but barely squeaked through with a *C-* average. Amy said she spoke five languages, and while that turned out to be true (Tagalog, her native dialect, Mandarin, Cantonese, and English), she couldn't speak any of them at anything higher than about a third-grade level. Walter found her conversation profoundly trivial with little interest in anything except friends and shopping. Walter was an accomplished musician; Amy had no comprehension of anything musical except what was locally popular. Walter was quiet and even-tempered; Amy was volatile and argumentative. Walter had been trained to be perceptive of other people's perspective. Amy had no idea that another perspective even existed. The list goes on and on.

Walter and Amy divorced after only seven weeks together—all spent on the other side of the world. The divorce was profoundly disturbing to Walter (they had both entered into the relationship in good faith), profoundly relieving (a life together was incomprehensible) and profoundly bewildering (how could he, an extremely bright, rational person, and presumably an expert in human relationships with a Ph.D. in sociology, ever become involved in such a mismatch?). The answer is the foundation of this book. In Walter's case the emotional biases (listed again below) had rendered an excellent brain totally dysfunctional. We restate the nine types of biases:

- **Intense need to get into a relationship**
- **Choices in the absence of knowledge**

- Intense love for an unsubstantiated image
- Belief in the accuracy of an image created without actual contact
- Choice without consultation with objective others
- Inoculation against any advice due to the certainty of choice
- Deception of others
- Self deception
- A feeling of entrapment

The unfortunate reality is that Walter's case is not unusual. I have met at least twenty people who have married through the same type of magazine that attracted Walter. Not one of the marriages has been successful. But the complaint is not against the magazine. There are millions of marriages that occur every year which operate under similar biases and produce similar disastrous results.

Let's Clear Your Thinking

At this point you are probably in agreement that as emotions increase the ability to think clearly diminishes. Most of you have experienced the pain of wanting to fulfill unmet healthy needs; the ache is practically physical, it's so strong. When emotions are extreme, clear thought largely disappears and which type of emotion you are experiencing makes little difference.

Thankfully there is help, even a solution. The path to clear thinking lies in remaining within a set of boundaries. The evidence of research psychology shows that the ability to set boundaries and adhere to them, particularly where strong emotions are involved, represents the foundation for success in many areas.[10] However, the time to draw such boundaries is long before the events that enflame emotions take place.

Remember my four-day trip to "Grama's" with my twins? *Now* when we travel, I *know* that taking an unplanned exit can wreak havoc with both the budget and time schedule, not to mention physical and emotional health. To prepare for such lures, I help the girls focus on the excitement of seeing Grama and talk about planning a different future trip that has the sole purpose of exploring a theme park or other such roadside attraction. As we successfully pass by the highway exit, we point with excitement at the bright lights and curlicue rides and what it will be like to go there and stay nearby. And afterwards, with my health, money and time well protected, I praise them (and myself) for pre-planning how to handle such an exciting temptation.

Don't let the call of the Sirens lure you to destruction. Make the choices that will ensure the likelihood of a long, satisfying and successful relationship.

Now, what I want you to do is take a deep breath because this is it. You're ready! The next section of the book focuses on giving you tools that will guide mutual conversations as you date and consider marriage. Be sure to look back at previous individual chapters as you run into hard decisions and temptations so that you can remind yourself of the value of rational choice. Because it is only with rational choice that you'll be free to enjoy and savor the sweet and exciting times of falling in love.

STEP THREE OF THE PRE*fix* PROCESS

Take a Look Together

DATING CONVERSATIONS

O kay. You now are officially ready to get back out there and start dating. You're armed with all the essentials; you know what you want and you're also aware of those things that can lure you off your course of finding "Mr. Right," and even disqualify the man sitting across from you at the restaurant. But, you still have a lot of men to actually meet to find that right guy. That might be a bit daunting for some of you.

To help, let me tell you a story. I'm sure most of you are familiar with Amway. They're one of the most successful multi-level marketing companies of all time. In their sales seminars, they use a great analogy, and one that is definitely useful for what we've been doing in this book. The seminar speaker asks the audience: if you *knew* that there were three perfect diamonds somewhere in a one-half mile gravel driveway, how many rocks would you look at to find those diamonds. The answer from some brave soul always is, "until I found all three diamonds—even if I had to go all the way to the end." The speaker then asks the audience, "what if we showed you ways that you didn't have to pick up all the rocks?" and everyone gets really excited. Of course they all want to know the shortcut.

Bringing the analogy back to relationships, let's say that to meet the perfect guy for you, you have to meet a hundred men. Do you have to look each and every one of them over carefully to figure out if they're a diamond or not? What if you could at least "short list" the group down to say ten or even five?

There are actually two ways you can meet the one "diamond" in the bunch. The first way is to go out with all of them over time, inadvertently using fairy-tale criteria to figure out as you go along whether each is a good fit or not. This, by the way, is how I went about dating for years! And while you have all the best intentions in the world to find the guy that best fits you, there is a huge problem with this approach. Because you aren't aware of all the pitfalls that can get in the way of making an informed decision, it's likely you won't meet all one hundred men. Just like when people are building a network marketing organization they often quit before they find their three diamonds, even though it is a fact that they are out there. You're going to get diverted at some point and follow your emotions, falling "in love" with no rational thinking behind it. Because you will not meet all of the possible suitors, you'll end up in a wrong relationship early on and your chances of it working out are about what the divorce rate is today: 50/50.

The other way to find your diamond is to use the elements of the compatibility code I'm sharing with you in this book. Remember, the first element of the code is to deconstruct the myth that has scripted your dating decisions up to this point. The second element is to apply all the principles and guidelines in the entire pre*fix* process. The set of criteria that I encouraged you to develop in "Take a Look Outward" allowed you to narrow the field down to a short list. We emphasized that if you meet someone with a disqualifier, you exhibit fortitude and check him off. You also know that you must be aware of potential biasers—strong emotions or an overwhelming need for physical closeness, for example—that can trip you up. But for the not so obvious qualities that you are seeking, you are going to need to have some more in-depth conversations, the subject of which is the third step of the pre*fix* process: "Take a Look Together."

Using the diamond example above, you may not recognize that the rock you picked up is indeed a precious stone, so you're going to need to brush off some of the dirt, get below the surface roughness, to find the beauty underneath. This step is all about the type of conversations that will help you determine if the person you are dating is a good match for you. It is also about developing communication patterns that will help to develop and maintain a successful marriage. There are four things that you need to find out about each other:

1. *Do your essence qualities match his?*

   Our seminar participants find that matching essence qualities is quite intriguing. It's like you're going on a treasure hunt, with the goal of finding out how well you are matched with the guy sitting across from you. Most people work together to identify their matching essences and as they do so it allows them to come to these conclusions:

   • Some couples discover they match well, so they rationally and consciously decide to continue the relationship and in many instances got married.

   • Some see there are challenge areas and have decided that even though they were deep into a relationship (some were even engaged and had wedding dates set) they decided to delay their plans for a year. Some eventually got married but others broke the relationship off because they found that their challenge areas were too difficult to overcome.

   • Other people have found that doing these exercises in this section was like having ice water dumped on them. These couples agreed that their differences were too great and that it would lead to constant stress. It took the emotional response out of the equation, and the couples were able to break up knowing that they were doing the right thing. In many of these instances the heartache caused by breaking up was dramatically lessened in the face of the peace from the rightfulness of the decision.

2. *What are your red flags and how do you deal with them?*

   The second matter that will stimulate many conversations are the areas we call *red flags*—literally those "hmmm, I don't know about that" kind of thing that should act as warnings to you. These are areas of potential incompatibility, things like, "he likes everything to be tidy and in its place," or "she is disorderly." I have recently counseled one couple, Anne and Bob, who have been dealing with this red flag for the past six years of their marriage. Some days the problem is more severe than others, and it is the underlying cause of 95 percent of their arguments. This highlights the importance of the red flags you face. While they don't necessarily cause you to call off the relationship, you must accept the fact that, by getting involved with this individual, you are will have to deal with the issues, in greater or lesser degree, for the rest of your life.

3. and 4. Are you both willing to contribute to a give-give relationship and live a life of shared purpose?

The third and forth aspects of a successful relationship are delightfully related and are presented as the third element of the compatibility code in the conclusion of this book. If you are reading this using the short-course format, I hope you will still turn to the last chapter and read about the keys to relationships that have wonderful beginnings *and* endings. There we explore the pivotal secrets of marriages that are really exceptional. They are respectively, having a give-give relationship and living a life of shared purpose.

It is because I truly want you to find a life-mate instead of suffering another broken heart; it is because I want you to write your very own "happily-ever-after" script that I warn you so strongly about what doesn't work. But I think you'll realize that as you work towards developing what "give-give" means to you personally in your relationship and discovering a life of shared purpose, you will find that your relationship truly can be the one of your dreams.

* Chapter 10 *

MATCHING OF ESSENCE QUALITIES
Creating Synergy that Lasts a Lifetime

L et's take inventory for a moment. You now have a good idea of who you are and what's important to you. You also have a list of biasers and sirens that you know how to sidestep, and most important, you have your shopping list ready. In fact, it's highly likely that you have had a few initial dates with someone and are looking for further insight on whether the two of you have a future together. Wherever you are on the relationship continuum, you don't want to miss what I'm going to teach you in this chapter for it gives you the most fundamental mechanism for determining compatibility.

You already know what essence qualities are. I hope that you have been adding to and clarifying your list as you've been reading. Once you have found a strong candidate for your life partner award, you get to go on what I like to think of as a treasure hunt, by mutually discovering and discussing each other's essence qualities. To do this, you'll need to encourage your guy to go through the same written processes you did in chapters 5 and 6, "The Straight Truth About Self" and "Discovering

Essence Qualities." For in order to find out how well you match, you need him to first document his own personal qualities and uncover his unique essence qualities.

I've included the worksheets, the ones you filled out in chapters 5 and 6, at the end of this chapter to make it easier for him to do the same work that you did. If you are far enough along in your dating process to think that you want to get serious with this man and he feels the same about you, then he will happily agree to do this. If he doesn't, it shows you that he has a resistance to working collectively and collaboratively on relational growth. Remember, a good marriage is one where the couple is constantly "working on it," and they should devote time each day or each week to learning more about each other as well as ways to enhance their relationship. It may take some coaxing, but I don't think so, especially if you present the whole process in the right way. I've had an amazing number of men come up to me and tell me that they want to meet the women who have read this book and have done the work I'm recommending here. I think they like the idea of a "process." If your guy flat-out refuses, consider it a disqualifier and, no matter how painful it is, move on. You've already done too much work on yourself for the relationship to be one-sided, and it serves as a herald of a dismal future where you will want to work on things and he will be passive or resistant.

Once your partner has identified his "Personal Qualities" and his "Individual Essences" you begin the fascinating process of finding out what matches, what really matters to each of you, and start the journey of discovering who you are together. As you do, know that your two lists of very unique essence qualities are not going to match item by item—nor should they. Essentially all people have differences, and the discussions that emerge regarding your non-matching essences will typically determine the future success of your relationship.

The treasure in these conversations will be the foundation to an understanding of each other that will build to the creation of a marvelous marriage. Let me tell you a story to show you what I mean. In the eight years that I've been married to Darren, I can remember many times that in the midst of an argument we were either focused on a subject that was laden with emotional issues or we were dealing with misunderstandings. All we needed to do to get out of the argument was to go back and focus again on the very things that brought us together, the foundational essences that we share. It reminds us, always, why we are together in the first place, and it also reinstates our shared purposes. There's a myriad of benefits to having matched your essences well. These essences become the common basis for the shared traditions, shared meaning, and shared purposes we pointed out in chapter 2 on the ideal marriage. My favorite benefit of this process is that by understanding Darren's essences, I am able to recognize what is very most important to him and to encourage him to grow as an individual.

But why delay? Let's get on to the specifics of how essences are matched.

HOW DO YOU MATCH ESSENCE QUALITIES?

There are some specific steps that you need to take, both separately and together, to do the matching exercise thoroughly. I'm going to go through it step-by-step to make it easy. In order to begin, you will both need your lists of essence qualities. You don't even have to show them to each other at this point as the first two steps are done separately. As I go through each step, I'm going to give you examples, both real and hypothetical, to help you understand the process.

Step One: Rank Ordering Your Essences

The first thing that you need to do is to individually rank your essence qualities in terms of importance. When you initially created your respective lists, it wasn't important to rank the items; you just needed to identify them and acknowledge their importance in your central definition. However, now that you are using your list to determine compatibility, the rank ordering allows you to place relative value on each of your essences. The higher ranked items obviously carry greater weight or importance. The lower items, in the context of an actual relationship, may be slightly modifiable without personal loss.

This first step also has an added benefit. As you rank them, you may find that some of the items on your list are not that strong and would be better defined as "interests" rather than essences.

The rank-ordering process can be difficult because most of your essences are vitally important and it is difficult to pick which ones are more important. This is what we might call a "fuzzy exercise" because precision is impossible. Do you rank your career more important than your family? The simple truth is that they are both vital. Handle this by positioning them near the top and ranked close together.

The important point here is that when you are finished rank ordering your entire list, you will know that items at the top of the list are more important than items at the bottom of the list. There is no merit in precisely determining whether items ranked number three and number four should be reversed, and as you start matching essence qualities with your partner, you will see why the precise number is unimportant.

Before I have you rank order your lists individually, we're going to start with a hypothetical example involving Harry and Sally (with apologies to Billy Crystal and Meg Ryan of *When Harry Met Sally* fame). They have each taken their essence qualities and filled in the Rank Order Chart:

RANK ORDER CHART Her List	
Name: Sally	
1.	Devout Christian
2.	Professor of Business
3	Outgoing and vivacious
4.	Loves Music
5.	Snuggler and romantic
6.	Accomplishment oriented
7.	Loves children
8.	
9.	
10	

RANK ORDER CHART His List	
Name: Harry	
1.	Fervent Christian
2.	Professor of Sociology
3	Plays Piano
4.	Logical Thinker
5.	Maintains a high level of fitness
6.	Affectionate
7.	Loves the Outdoors
8.	Entrepreneurial
9.	Decisive
10.	

Now it's you're turn. I've provided worksheets for you and your partner at the end of the chapter.

Step Two: Matching Your Qualities

Now that you have an idea of how your qualities rank, you're ready to start the matching process. I've developed a chart to help you work through these conversations with each other, building from the lists you created in previous chapters. We'll continue to have Sally and Harry help us as I walk you though the directions on using the "Matching Based on Essence Qualities" chart. You'll also find a blank version reproduced at the end of this chapter for you and your partner to use.

The first thing you do, allowing ladies to go first, is take your personal rank-ordered list of essences and put them in the left hand column, in order from first to last. Next, look at his rank-ordered list and discuss which of his essences are clear, obvious matches with yours. They don't have to be identical, but they do need to deal with the same issues. With Sally and Harry there were two essences that deal with similar issues: fervent Christian/devout Christian; snuggly and romantic/affectionate; Professor of Business/Professor of Sociology; loves music/plays piano. As you place his essences on the sheet, write them out beside the closest match with yours. At this point you'll notice that his ranking is probably out of order and that there are blank spaces where there are no similar matches available. This is natural, and we'll go over how to consider the implications of this in the next steps. For now, you just need to see where there are matches and where there aren't. Your final part of Step Two is to write down the remainder of those qualities from his essence list in his column and this chart across from blank spaces in yours, using his ranking numbers to determine the order. You'll see what I mean on Sally and Harry's chart on the next page; also notice that there are three more empty columns that we work with in later steps.

Matching Based on Essence Qualities

Her name: *Sally*   His name: *Harry*

Her Essences	Rank	His Essences	Rank	Identifying the type of match*	Her encour-agement of him **	His encour-agement of her **
Devout Christian	#1	Fervent Christian	#1			
Prof of Business	#2	Prof of Sociology	#2			
Outgoing and vivacious	#3					
Loves Music	#4	Plays piano	#3			
Snuggler and romantic	#5	Affectionate	#6			
Accomplish-ment oriented	#6					
Loves children	#7					
		Logical thinker	#4			
		Maintains high level fitness	#5			
		Loves the outdoors	#7			
		Entre-preneurial	#8			
		Decisive	#9			

℞ *Step Three: Identifying the Type of Match*

As you just found out, the essence lists you created earlier will almost never include the same items as your partner's, and you may have had difficulty figuring out whether your items matched or not. This is typical, and to take you into the next stage of conversation, Darren and I have created a category system that helps you begin to consider what a life together might look like. When you both have an identical item listed as an essence—or a closely related item—these are all classed as "clear matches." When an essence on one of the charts has no match with an essence on your partner's chart, these would be identified as an "adapted match," a "challenged match," or a "non-match." While the clear match is easy to see, the remaining three categories can help you figure out how to classify your unmatched essences. We clarify below:

A. **Clear match**: The couple lists the same (or closely related) quality as an essence and they match well within the context of that quality.

B. **Adapted match**: These are areas in which an essence listed for one is not listed for the other. Typically the partner has a similar but less dominant quality in this area. For instance, he breeds and trains dogs (an essence) and she enjoys dogs (an interest).

C. **Challenged match**: These are also areas in which an essence listed for one is not listed for the other. This means that the partner does not relate to it at all or possesses opposite attitudes or interest in that area. For instance, he is former college basketball star and a season ticket holder to Los Angeles Lakers games; she has no interest and has been disgusted with the out-of control salaries of professional athletes. This may require significant, sometimes painful adjustments to find an acceptable solution.

D. **Non-Match/Disqualifier**: These are also areas in which an essence listed for one is not listed for the other. A true non-match means the differences are too great or the essences are actually antagonistic to each other. For instance, someone who heads up the National Stop-Smoking Campaign is not going to marry someone who smokes or owns a tobacco farm. These are in fact disqualifiers and typically end the relationship.

There is no formula to tell how many of which type of matches will result in success. Each individual has different tolerances for non-matches. There are also no hard and fast rules about what ratio of A's (Clear matches), B's (Adapted matches) and C's (Challenged matches) creates a successful marriage. However, I have found that a single D will break the relationship, and a single C puts the relationship at risk. A couple can sometimes thrive despite a single C-ranked item perhaps even two of them, but this would require a mature couple with effective negotiating skills. Exceptional marriages are typically composed primarily of A's and B's.

Now, obviously it is fairly easy to see the A's and even the D's on a chart. With Sally and Harry, they had a couple of obvious clear matches. Fortunately, they don't have any D's, but let's consider what might have created some. For example, Harry loves the out-of-doors, but if Sally really resisted anything more primitive than camping at the Hilton they would probably have a *D*; we'll look later at how they determined that this was not a *D* as we work through Step Four on "Encouragement." Next, notice that Sally loves children and Harry does not have a matching essence in his column. If the absence of something about children on his list is because he doesn't want to have children of his own, then they have a *D*. A dear friend of mine found herself in this situation and thought that there were enough other positive things about her boyfriend that she could let the children essence go from her life. They married, and as the years went by her desire for children increased, but his remained at zero. Today, after a painful divorce caused by a variety of reasons, she is approaching fifty and the window in her life for bearing her own children has closed, leaving emptiness, heartache, and regret.

Moving back into the shadowy area of *B*'s and *C*'s, you'll find that most of your pre-marriage and early marriage conversations will revolve around these because both types require accommodation and planning. Remember, we're dealing with *the* things that are the most important to each of you, and in the event that the other person does not share interests in particular essences, you must consider the consequences. I've been promising you since the Preface that I would provide you with dating conversations, and here's one of the biggies. It's only by talking about the blank spaces on the chart that you find out where, how and if you fit.

For example, if Sally says: "gosh, look at this. One of my essences is outgoing and vivacious. I've even ranked its importance to me at "number three," but there's no corresponding essence on your side. What do you think about outgoing and vivacious people, Harry?"

Harry might come back and say, "I love being around someone who's outgoing and vivacious. I'm not that way, obviously, but that's okay." This clarifies the type of match as "adapted," a *B*. Now if Harry's answer to Sally's question is "You know, when people are outspoken, it embarrasses me," then the match is either a *C* or a *D*, and only through clarification will Sally figure out which one it is.

Remember, if you determine that this particular area is a *D*, you have to seriously consider if it is a disqualifier. If you figure out that you have a *C*, then Step Four will help you to start identifying how much of a risk it is to your future relationship by determining how willing or not you are to encourage and participate in those areas that are not clear matches.

Let's take a look at what Sally and Harry wrote down after "identifying the type of match."

Matching Based on Essence Qualities

Her name: Sally   His name: Harry

Her Essences	Rank	His Essences	Rank	Identifying the type of match*	Her encouragement of him **	His encouragement of her **
Devout Christian	#1	Fervent Christian	#1	A		
Prof of Business	#2	Prof of Sociology	#2	A		
Outgoing and vivacious	#3			B		
Loves Music	#4	Plays piano	#3	A		
Snuggler and romantic	#5	Affectionate	#6	A		
Accomplishment oriented	#6			B		
Loves children	#7			B		
		Logical thinker	#4	B		
		Maintains high level fitness	#5	C		
		Loves the outdoors	#7	C		
		Entrepreneurial	#8	B		
		Decisive	#9	B		

*Type of Match Rating:
A – clear match
B – adapted match
C – challenged match
D – non-match/disqualifier

℞ *Step Four: Identifying the Degree of Encouragement*

The final two columns of the chart might look confusing at first, but as I said in the last step, this is where you really determine the impact or consequences of your differences, and consider if you are mutually willing to work on overcoming those differences. Remember the concertmaster and the cowboy that I told you about in the chapter on disqualifiers? She wanted a quiet home; he wanted one bursting with people. They discovered that they couldn't overcome that difference as they did this step. It became a deal breaker that helped them to see that their relationship wouldn't work.

This section of the chart is where the bulk of your dating conversations happen because not only are you figuring out what your mismatches represent, you are also trying to envision what encouragement and participation in each other's essences mean. Two prominent questions come up in my seminars as I am frequently asked: 1) *how will marriage influence each of the partner's essences,* and 2) looking down the road twenty, thirty, or forty years, *how will our relationship change these core essence qualities with the passage of time?* Usually marriage will either enhance the other person's essences or detract from them. It is rare for the relationship to exert no influence at all.

Essence qualities are much too rich and diverse to fit into a simple formula; however, to help get you started thinking and talking about how you are going to negotiate your similarities and differences, I provide you with the following rating guide as a starting point. In this stage of conversations I want you to consider the degree of encouragement, support and participation that you would engage in on the essence qualities that your partner listed. Notice that you will rate your degree of encouragement for each of your partner's essences. The guide is displayed on the next page so you can see them as I talk about them. I also include the guide at the bottom of Sally and Harry's fully filled-out chart that comes at the end of this step.

As you read down the list, you see that there are varying degrees of encouragement, each modified by two or three categories of participation. In your conversations, you need to talk about how much you are willing to encourage each other in your essence qualities, and if you want to participate in them or not. As you talk, and as you'll see in the examples I provide in a moment, be reassured that a happy marriage doesn't necessarily mean that you have to fully participate in all your partner's essence qualities.

Here's the list of "Encouragement by Partner Rating:"

E1 – Enthusiastic encouragement—full participation

E2 – Enthusiastic encouragement —partial participation

E3 – Generous encouragement—full participation

E4 – Generous encouragement—partial participation

E5 – Generous encouragement—little or no participation

E6 – Partial encouragement—partial participation

E7 – Partial encouragement—little or no participation

E8 – Little or no encouragement—partial participation

E9 – Little or no encouragement—little or no participation

E10 – Passive irritation

E11 – Active antagonism

Looking at some real life examples from my own marriage might help you make distinctions in your rating decisions. Here they are:

- **Example of an *E1* Rating (enthusiastic encouragement, full participation).** When Darren and I married we were both in love with music. I was thrilled to sing in the Briarwood Presbyterian Church Choir, a large and talented group often accompanied by full orchestra. Darren's background was piano and trombone, particularly the trombone where he, over the years, played in bands, orchestras, and a number of smaller ensemble groups. Darren played and toured with the university band, and immediately after we married I considered singing in the university choir. However, as I told you before, I decided I would learn the French horn so I could participate with Darren—something I could not do if I sang in the choir. Six years later, Darren and I play and tour with a chamber orchestra. We also encouraged this passion in my twins as we modeled both the love and discipline of music to them. At Christmas we all haul our instruments to Alabama and play along with the Christmas carols while others sing. Today, both girls (in the seventh grade as of this writing) play the trumpet and are good enough that all four of us play and tour with the university band. Not only did I participate in Darren's essence quality, but I also challenged him to improve. I'll ask Darren to tell the now legendary story in our family in his own words:

> I played trombone pretty well but one day Elizabeth said, "You want to play that thing good?" Irritated, I responded, "I already play pretty good." Elizabeth said, "You want to play that thing good?" More irritated, I again responded, "I already play pretty good." Once more with prickly disdain she said, "You want to *really* play that thing good?" I understood. I joined the Ritchie Trombone Choir the following month, and a year later began to take lessons from the principal trombonist of a highly respected symphony orchestra. Four years later I am principal trombone in the Ritchie Group and frequently solo with a number of different ensembles. Recently my teacher said, "You have acquired all the skills of a professional, and while they need to continue to be developed and applied more consistently, you are at the top of the heap among amateur trombonists in Alberta."

- **Example of an *E2* Rating (enthusiastic encouragement, partial participation).** After I moved to Canada to be with Darren, I taught in the School of Business at Canadian University College for six years. During my sixth-year there, Darren and I discussed the idea of my becoming a full time public speaker and consultant. Despite the fear of having our family income cut in half, Darren was fully supportive of the move and continued to be encouraging even when my income was unstable. As an *E2* rating suggests, while providing enthusiastic encouragement, he could not fully participate because he was not a public speaker. He would attend my speeches when his schedule allowed, which I appreciated, but it was more important to me that he kept encouraging me as I worked to become a successful entrepreneur.

- **Example of an *E7* Rating (partial encouragement, little or no participation).** Darren was a nationally ranked runner in his youth. His 2:20:10 marathon was eleventh fastest in the U.S. in 1972. He has continued to enjoy track and field and coaches local high school athletes in cross-country and track. I have no intrinsic interest in track and field, but when Darren expresses concern to me about whether his coaching involvement is perhaps taking too much time away from family, I encourage him to continue. When the 2001 World Championships of Track and Field were hosted by Edmonton, just an hour up the road from us, I pooled the resources of family members who chipped in to buy him a full ten-day pass. He enjoyed every moment; I did not attend, which was okay with him. But he knows that I am fully supportive of this specific interest of his.

The first seven levels of encouragement typically represent an excellent encouragement response to the essence qualities of one's partner. Numbers *E8* and *E9* are also acceptable in certain cases. Please don't burden your relationship with the expectation of having to enjoy everything together. Darren and I do in fact have several qualities that we score somewhere between an *E8* and an *E9*. I'll give you an example of an *8/9* rating to show you that even when something looks insurmountable, it can be dealt with, as long as there's a lot of love and no small amount of thought and humor put into it.

- **Example of an *E8/E9* Rating (little or no encouragement and reluctant participation).** Here's the story: I love animals, but I haven't had a pet for many, many years. Being a single mother with twin daughters and moving fairly often was not conducive to pets. Darren and I discussed pets before we married and, while he likes animals, he feels that they must have the proper environment; having a pet depends on how and where you live. Eventually, we did get a cat. Our very independent cat fit well with our incredibly active lifestyle. But, over the years, there has always been the matter of "the dog." The twins and I wanted a dog. After all, I had spent several years (before children) training and owning Labrador Retrievers, and while Darren loves dogs he thinks you need to live in the country on five acres to own anything that woofs. Every time he would say this, the twins would moan: "by the time you own five acres and a house, we're going to be married and gone. We want a dog while we're still kids!" The impasse lasted until this past summer when my very smart daughters who studied their stepfather well produced a PowerPoint presentation explaining why a golden retriever was the perfect dog for our environmental and financial circumstances. Darren, the logical researcher and academician, knew when he had been beaten at his own game. We are now the proud owners of a lovely golden retriever, Amber, and while things are going well, this scenario still definitely ranks as an *E8* or *E9*. Darren gives us little or no encouragement, but he will participate by running or "loving on" the dog when her soulful eyes beg for his attention. He doesn't like the fact that Amber doesn't have a farm to run on, but he's a softy at heart, and Amber's got some pretty eloquent eyes.

- **Warning:** *E10/E11* **Equal Disqualifiers**

  Now, the two areas that are absolutely unacceptable are numbers *E10* (passive irritation) and *E11* (active antagonism). If you are irritated or antagonistic about something that is an essence quality of your partner, it is best to find out long before you are married and break off the relationship. The disturbing reality is that there are millions of marriages that are characterized by irritation and antagonism. I'm certain that with very little thought, images of a few such marriages spring to mind.

BACK TO SALLY AND HARRY

Now that I've given you some things to think about given my own experiences, let's go back to Sally and Harry's progress. They spent many hours talking about what their essence qualities really meant; what did "affectionate" mean for Harry and how did that jive with what Sally thought about affection, for instance. They had fun doing it. People love to talk about themselves, and as they discovered more about each other, that led to additional questions, more discussions, and ultimately, a deepening of their love.

Here's their fully completed chart so you know what they discovered. I'll conclude by giving you a peek into their discussions about how they would handle some of their mismatches.

Matching Based on Essence Qualities

Her name: *Sally*   His name: *Harry*

Her Essences	Rank	His Essences	Rank	Identifying the type of match*	Her encouragement of him **	His encouragement of her **
Devout Christian	#1	Fervent Christian	#1	A	E1	E1
Prof of Business	#2	Prof of Sociology	#2	A	E2	E2
Outgoing and vivacious	#3			B		E6
Loves Music	#4	Plays piano	#3	A	E2	E2
Snuggler and romantic	#5	Affectionate	#6	A	E1	E1
Accomplish-ment oriented	#6			B		E1
Loves children	#7			B		E1
		Logical thinker	#4	B	E4	
		Maintains high level fitness	#5	C	E5	
		Loves the outdoors	#7	C	E6	
		Entre-preneurial	#8	B	E2	
		Decisive	#9	B	E4	

*Type of Match Rating:
A – clear match
B – adapted match
C – challenged match
D – non-match/

**Encouragement by Partner Rating
E1 – Enthusiastic encouragement—full participation
E2 – Enthusiastic encouragement—partial participation
E3 – Generous encouragement-full participation
E4 – Generous encouragement-partial disqualifier participation
E5 – Generous encouragement-little or no participation
E6 – Partial encouragement-partial participation
E7 – Partial encouragement-little or no participation
E8 – Little or no encouragement-partial participation
E9 – Little or no encouragement-little or no participation
E10 – Passive irritation
E11 – Active antagonism

Some of the differences that they had to deal with were quite amusing. Take Harry's high level of fitness and his love for the outdoors. He personally ranked them #5 and #7 respectively. They quickly found that these were both areas of "challenged matches," but they were willing to take a look and see if they could come up with any workable solutions. Here's what they decided:

Harry "maintains a high level of fitness," runs every day, does pull ups, makes efforts to eat well, takes nutritionals, and maintains close to an ideal weight. The topic is not listed for Sally, thus her encouragement rating of *E5* ("generous encouragement, little or no participation"). She actually exercises about once a year and admits to hating every moment. If the attitudes are extreme this difference could lead to parallel lives depending on the level of obsession on Harry's part and the level of disgust or antagonism on Sally's. The reality is that Sally encourages Harry in all his health efforts and thoroughly enjoys being married to a fit individual. Further, there are some matches as Sally is weight conscious, eats healthfully, and plans to initiate a regular exercise program, as long as she is allowed to hate it! Despite surface differences, it turns out to be an area of non-conflict. Sally does struggle with conflicting emotions between knowing what her fitness level ought to be and her negative attitudes toward exercise. Harry, though, is not out to find a running buddy, and they encourage each other to eat right, maintain ideal weight, and work toward good health. Even without verbal conflict, however, these differences represent significant opposing life patterns and the couple will need to be aware of potential problems.

The lowest ranked item is a potential non-match. It involves Harry's love of the outdoors. Sally does not address this issue (her *E6* rating means "partial encouragement, partial participation"), but the couple shares a true difference here. Sally decidedly enjoys civilization with all its amenities and has never particularly taken to sleeping on sharp rocks, suffering the choking smoke of campfires, enduring the swarms of mosquitoes, the freezing cold baths, the inconsistent meals, or the layer of grit that is ever present. Harry enjoys civilization well enough but absolutely loves the outdoors. The telling gauge will be how extreme are the differences. If Harry's love of the outdoors is obsessive, (say for example he wants to make their residence on the top of Sulfur Mountain, haul in water for a stream one-half mile away, build an outhouse for their daily ablutions, and live off the land), and Sally is on the low end, (her idea of "roughing it" is a night at Motel 6), the relationship is doomed. If they marry, they will live parallel lives.

Because Sally and Harry were able to find areas of compatibility that worked for both of them what had potential to be a non-match turned out to be quite congenial. They looked carefully at what Sally didn't like about camping and identified ways to eliminate or minimize her objections: an air mattress blunts sharp rocks, a good fire doesn't smoke so much, mosquito repellants come in a variety of fragrances, and baths are not so objectionable if you avoid glacier-fed streams. What started as a challenged match, possibly even a non-match, was satisfactorily resolved for both of them. But, make no mistake; it will take unselfish commitment toward each other and many conversations across the years to make the gap manageable.

SUCCESSFUL AND UNSUCCESSFUL RESOLUTION OF ESSENCE QUALITY DIFFERENCES

Before I let you loose and have you start working on your Matching Essence chart, I want to give you one more way of looking at the sticky issue of whether or not a couple can successfully negotiate essence differences. Darren, my hubby the psychologist, has found that there are three factors that come into play. They are:

1. Magnitude of difference
2. Willingness to change
3. Maturity of the couple

℞

What follows are six contrasting pairs of couples who are attempting to resolve substantial essence quality differences. As you read, notice how the three items listed above (magnitude of difference, willingness to change, maturity of the couple) influence success or non-success in these areas.

Acceptable resolution achieved	Acceptable resolution NOT achieved
1 ☺Andre is a concert pianist and practices three to four hours a day. Ruby has little musical talent but supports his practice and performance schedule, spends time learning more about music, attends all his concerts, and makes every effort to be supportive of his growth as a musician.	1a ☹Marc is a concert pianist and practices three to four hours a day. Vanessa has little musical talent, finds his endless practice of scales and arpeggios slowly driving her crazy, suggests that he find somewhere else to practice, does not attend his concerts and makes little effort to understand Marc's world.
2 ☺Alicia is a researcher in the field of psychology; her partner, Garrick, is neither psychologically or mathematically inclined but reads her write-ups (despite some gaps of knowledge in the analysis sections), discusses with pleasure some of the findings, and develops a growing interest and awareness of her area of expertise.	2a ☹Amanda is a prominent Ph.D. physicist who takes ultimate pleasure in researching the mysteries of the universe. She is dating a handsome hunk with the IQ of a cabbage. The hunk does not have the resources to ever appreciate the brilliant mind (and hence the world) of his partner.
3 ☺A young couple discusses having children. Karla grew up in a warm, nurturing home and wants several children; Daniel was an only child and would actually prefer to have no children. He has never particularly enjoyed the mini-critters but decides to assist in the local elementary school once a week and discovers a growing fascination with the little tykes. Eventually he grows to the point that a family with children is something he realizes he can embrace and enjoy.	3a ☹Ellie wants children, Allen doesn't. Because he loves Ellie he tries the same trick as his innovative counterpart, Daniel. In every contact with young 'uns he realizes how incompatible his nature is with the smelly, clamoring, noisy little brats. He finds himself unable to embrace a marriage that involves devoting 20-25 years of his life to bringing them up.
	Chart continued on next page…

...Chart continued from previous page	
4 ☺Anna is an agnostic who has little interest in spiritual things. Paul is a deeply committed Christian. Both want children and realize that the spiritual contrast would not be good for their family. Anna knows that Paul is not going to give up or seriously alter his beliefs so she begins to study with the local pastor, reads books like C. S. Lewis' *Surprised by Joy*, begins to attend church with Paul, and eventually nurtures her spiritual side into a full commitment that integrates into Paul's spiritual world.	4a ☹Susie is an agnostic who has little interest in spiritual things. Silas is a deeply committed Christian. Susie knows that Silas is not going to give up his spiritual beliefs. In spite of efforts on Susie's part to nurture a spiritual perspective she finds herself hardening into atheism and an increasing antagonism toward those associated with religion.
5 ☺Pam is a party animal who enjoys an active social life and derives energy when around other people. Dudley enjoys people but is quieter and prefers one-on-one contacts. He typically finds the party setting pointless and eventually tiring. However, Dudley is genuinely eager to become more social and Pam realizes that she would benefit by a reduction of her party fever—which has often gotten her into trouble in the past. Even with persistent effort, there is never a match of sociability, but Dudley learns to enjoy the occasional party, becomes genuinely more interested in social interactions and Pam learns to enjoy some of Dudley's quieter joys.	5a ☹Frizzle is a party animal who enjoys an active social life and derives energy when around other people. Marvin enjoys people but is quieter and prefers one-on-one contacts. He finds the party setting often pointless and eventually tiring. Frizzle's social activities are very important to her, her parties much too much fun to consider change. Marvin by contrast finds most parties a torment and no effort can shift that perspective. Even though they love each other, they eventually realize that an integrated life is not possible.
	Chart continued on next page...

...Chart continued from previous page	
Acceptable resolution achieved	Acceptable resolution NOT achieved
6 ☺Anthony is a triathlete who pursues his obsession with fierce determination and crams two hours a day into training despite a full time job. His wife, Elly, was a rower in her college days and pursued the sport for several years beyond graduation. Despite the different sports, she understands the fascination with achievement and the daily grit and discipline required for success. Elly herself pursues an active lifestyle, runs and bikes with her husband from time to time and attends and supports him during his three or four competitive efforts each year.	6a ☹Gunther is a triathlete who pursues his obsession with fierce determination and crams two hours a day into training despite a full time job. His partner, Michelle, has never pursued athletics (or any other keen passion for that matter), cannot comprehend how anyone could be so obsessed with such a pointless activity, is terminally unfit herself and has no interest either in participating with him or going to his competitions.

So let's take a look at the dynamics of some of the differences and changes described above.

The gap was too great: In some instances the mismatch is so great that no effort on the part of the non-essence partner could make a significant difference. These include Amanda (2a) the Ph.D. physicist; Frizzle (5a) the party animal; and Michelle (6a) who was disgusted with triathlons. It would be the incredibly rare couple who could close such large gaps.

Efforts at change were unsuccessful: We consider Allen (3a) who disliked children or Susie (4a) the agnostic who tried to develop a spiritual perspective. Both made a sincere effort to change but their attempts were unsuccessful. This represents an individual difference factor. Just across the page successful partners began with the same challenge. Why was one set of people successful whereas another set was unsuccessful? The answer is deeply rooted in one's personal makeup. Whatever the reasons, these questions need to be answered before a couple joins their lives together.

No effort was made: This leaves us with Vanessa (1a) who was irritated at Marc's piano playing and made no effort (either through ignorance or laziness) to integrate this important quality into her life. Her successful counterpart, Ruby (1), not only realized that it was important to be supportive of Andre's musical efforts, but made the choice to become actively involved.

Successful effort was made: For the six couples, a successful resolution was accomplished. In each of these six cases it involved 1) the willingness to change; 2) the ability to change; and 3) the maturity of the person that allowed them to make extraordinary efforts to encourage and support their partner.

As you embark on your negotiations—the wonderful conversations you will have with your partner—you will get tested sometimes. There will be things that come up that you don't like. It is entirely up to you to decide if that makes the item a disqualifier.

I envy you in a way. Writing this brings back so many memories. Sometimes, when Darren and I were at a seeming impasse on an issue, it really helped me to see some of the more hidden sides of Darren as we worked to solve them. Some of the conversations we had were downright hilarious, and in the end, these exercises helped create an even stronger bond between us. But, I also know from long experience that sometimes there are unbridgeable differences on essence issues that no amount of effort can resolve. The only comfort I can give you is that because you've recognized them early on, it can save the heartbreak down the road. Just know that the wisdom to be found in each of the cases listed above, is that *the more passive we are about our partner's essence qualities, the more we risk living parallel rather than integrated lives.*

With parallel lives the relationship becomes more distant and the risk of a break becomes increasingly likely. That is exactly what I don't want to happen in your relationship. It goes back to the basic tenet of the book: choose wisely. I'm also well aware that you may have uncovered a few issues that you're not quite sure what to do with. That's what we take up in the next chapter. Those issues are likely to be red flags, those things that you know are potential problems, but you're not yet equipped to deal with them. For now, I ask that you do the matching essences exercise so that you can be aware of your similarities and in the event of differences, actively decide if they can be overcome. If they can, then enjoy the process of growth that you go through as you each work to accommodate and eventually celebrate the other's essences. I'm sure that you will cry some, laugh a lot, and develop that deep, rich, lasting love that keeps marriages together and happy.

His Personal Characteristics

Name: _____ Date: _____

Category	Change Desired	Personal Quality or Characteristic
Social & Relational		
Family		
Spiritual & Philosophical		
Temperament & Personality		
Personal Habits		
		Chart continued on next page...

...Chart continued from previous page		
Interests & Passions		
Intellectual, Vocational & Financial		
Physical Characteristics		
Health & Fitness		
Contributions & Service		
Other Areas		

His Individual Essence Qualities Worksheet

Name: _____ Date: _____

Note: List qualities of greater strength or importance toward top

Essence Qualities

RANK ORDER CHART
Her List
Name:
1.
2.
3.
4.
5.
6.
7.
8.
9.
10.

RANK ORDER CHART
His List
Name:
1.
2.
3.
4.
5.
6.
7.
8.
9.
10.

Matching Based on Essence Qualities

Her name: _____ His name: _____

Her Essences	Rank	His Essences	Rank	Identifying the type of match*	Her encouragement of him **	His encouragement of her **

*Type of Match Rating:

A – clear match
B – adapted match
C – challenged match
D – non-match/

**Encouragement by Partner Rating

E1 – Enthusiastic encouragement—full participation
E2 – Enthusiastic encouragement—partial participation
E3 – Generous encouragement-full participation
E4 – Generous encouragement-partial disqualifier participation
E5 – Generous encouragement-little or no participation
E6 – Partial encouragement-partial participation
E7 – Partial encouragement-little or no participation
E8 – Little or no encouragement-partial participation
E9 – Little or no encouragement-little or no participation
E10 – Passive irritation
E11 – Active antagonism

Note: A full size chart is available for free download in your Bonus at: www.TheCompatibilityCode.com/bonus

Chapter 11

RED FLAGS

Perform Due Diligence;
Proceed with Caution!

Matching essences sure is enlightening, isn't it? I hope that you and your partner have spent many wonderful hours discovering each other; however, I bet this is what's going on. You've found some delightful ways in which you match essences, but you've come up against some things that you're not sure what to do with. You know these areas are going to cause problems, but you don't know how much. They don't look like disqualifiers, but they could be. What you're coming up against is a red flag. By definition, these are qualities, characteristics or circumstances of a person or couple that has the potential to jeopardize the success of that relationship. They aren't initially seen as deal breakers, although if the red flag is severe enough, or there are too many of them, you may choose to turn them into disqualifiers. If we use the diamond analogy we started this section with, all diamonds have flaws. It just depends on what level of magnification you use to find them. However, if the flaw is large enough—and in a diamond that means it is visible to the naked eye—it may render the gem unusable.

So too with red flags. No two people ever match perfectly. That would actually make for a boring marriage if you think about it. Rather, we bring ourselves, warts and all, to a relationship. We all have flaws, and all couples, even those in amazingly successful marriages, have red flags that need attention. The purpose of this chapter is to help you recognize what your red flags are and give you conversational tools to help you judge their importance, understand how severe they are, and judge how dangerous they may be to you as a couple.

First, you spend time finding out what some of your red flags are. I say "some" because red flags pop up all the time. The longer you spend together, the more you encounter situations, the greater awareness you have of these relational challenges.

Once you have identified some of your red flags you will then determine what to do with them. You may find that the differences between the two of you on a red-flag issue are so great that it becomes a disqualifier. Yes, I know you may be thinking: "Elizabeth, we devoted an entire chapter to disqualifiers. Do we have to do it again?" Let's be frank. The possibility of disqualification should last up right up to the moment when you say, "I do." The processes you go though as you date and determine the compatibility of a particular individual are not only step-by-step but are also fluid. Life is rarely black and white. If you determine that the conflict area you are discussing is not a deal breaker, it still remains between you as a challenge to be resolved.

TWO TYPES OF RED FLAGS

There are two classes of red flags:

1. Mismatches of personal qualities or characteristics; and
2. Risk factors that arise from external circumstances.

Mismatches of personal qualities can arise from either positive or negative personality traits and can be measured in terms of their degree of intensity. Take, for instance the quality of "I exhibit anger." This could be measured on a scale of "rarely" to "often."

The second class creates challenges due to the risk factors that arise from external circumstances reflecting facts that you cannot change. Sometimes they are events that were beyond your control, other times they are the results of your own past decisions. These risk factors are not necessarily negative in and of themselves, but their presence in a relationship definitely represents a red flag and therefore must be discussed and their potential impact considered. We will take these up in the latter part of this chapter.

Red Flags due to Mismatch of Personal Qualities

In this first section, whether qualities are positive or negative is not our concern, instead it is the contrast between the partners on a particular quality. The contrasting qualities themselves usually have a "versus" attached to it, such as "introvert versus extravert" or "couch potato versus fitness guru." Gary Chapman in *The Five Love Languages* has a great example of this. Babbling Brook and Dead Sea go out on a date. The dead-sea guy thinks, "This is perfect." He finds that he doesn't have to extend himself at all, yet has this interesting and vivacious woman paying attention to him. The babbling brook also thinks, "This is perfect," because she has an absorbed audience, who listens with avid interest. The problem is, ten years into the marriage, Mr. Dead Sea thinks: "Doesn't she ever shut up" and Ms. Babbling Brook thinks, "Is he ever going to say anything?" [1]

Examples of Mismatches That Create Red Flags   ℞

The question I hear many of you asking here is, "Can you give us some examples?" Certainly! Here is a list of common mismatches that we hope serve as models so that you can apply them to the red flags you find in your relationship. Some of them are obvious, mismatches you have seen many times. Others may have never crossed your mind. Remember, this is only a sampling.

- Intelligent vs. unintelligent
- High strung vs. placid & laid back
- extraverted vs. introverted
- Low psychic metabolism (low energy) vs. high psychic metabolism (high energy)

- Extraordinary talent (or accomplishment) vs. ordinary abilities & accomplishments
- Ambitious vs. content with status quo
- Attractive vs. unattractive
- Cultured vs. barbarian
- Spiritual vs. unspiritual (or different styles of spirituality)
- Philosophical vs. frivolous
- Risk taker vs. obsessed with safety
- Commitment to vigorous personal growth vs. content with the status quo
- Visionary vs. lives in the moment
- Scrupulously honest vs. morally flexible
- Wealth-acquisition mindset vs. poverty mindset
- Neat and organized vs. slovenly and disorganized
- Logical thinker vs. emotional, reactive thinker
- Couch potato vs. physically active
- Regular exercise regimen vs. none
- Involved in service outreaches vs. pursues only personal pleasuring
- Argumentative Andy vs. non-confrontational Carla
- Back packer Bert vs. five-star-hotel-connoisseur Connie
- Frugal Freddy vs. shop-'til-you-drop Shelley

It does not take a research psychologist to see the challenges some of these contrasts would inflict on a relationship. Later on (in the section titled "Classic Examples of Mismatches") we will explore several of these contrasts in detail. But next we will look at how you can determine the challenge red flags pose to your relationship by having you 1) identify your own red flags based on personality mismatches, and then 2) charting how much of a gap there is in the mismatch.

℞ FIRST IDENTIFY YOUR RED FLAGS

If you are currently in a relationship you have undoubtedly already found some mismatches, and it's smart to write them down. Other red flags may be discovered by considering the list of contrasts from the previous page or even looking at the list of personal qualities from your "Straight Truth About Self" exercise. To find your red flags, look at the list from that chapter, identify those that have a sense of "versus," or opposites, and see whether additional red flags emerge. In addition, you and your partner can brainstorm back and forth about differences you've noticed in your relationship. A worksheet is provided at the end of the chapter to assist in this process.

MEASURING THE SIGNIFICANCE OF THE RED FLAGS

It's one thing to identify your potential red flags; it's another thing entirely to figure out how much trouble they can potentially cause you and thus how much work you're going to have to put into preventing or handling the upsets that come from their presence.

There are three factors we use in combination to give us insight as to whether a particular set of red flags is going to yield insurmountable challenges to a particular relationship.

How great is the difference between the two of you? If you have ever worked with a percentile scale you'll know that they come in handy when you are trying to measure differences. In the extraversion example that we share with you later in the chapter, we estimate Darren at 40 percent on the scale and 95 percent for me. That represents a fifty-five-point difference (95 − 40 = 55), which provides an estimate of the gap we have in this area. You don't need to take a personality test to come with reasonable estimates of your position on a scale for most qualities. If you happen to have taken a test, fine, go ahead and make use of it

To measure contrasts in your personality traits, we will now go into more detail about the percentile scale like the one shown here:

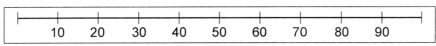

We've all seen them and know that a score of 50 means half the people are higher, half are lower. A score of 80 means 20 percent of people are higher and 80 percent are lower. If I were to ask you to place an X on the scale to indicate your level of extraversion (a 0 is very introverted, a 100, very extraverted), I'm sure you would have no trouble. The same would be true for many other qualities. In a moment, I'm going to ask you to rate your differences using the percentile scale. However, let me briefly discuss two additional factors.

How important is the issue to each of you? To help you understand this factor, take the religious discrepancy issue of "Pentecostal versus Methodist." If a couple is deeply committed to their individual faiths and the denominations represent seriously contrasting perspectives, the importance would be high. If they only enter a church for weddings and funerals, then different denominations might not be a problem at all.

How many of them are there? This is relatively self-explanatory. If you have too many, the relationship will be compromised if not doomed. How many is too many, of course, depends on the couple and the severity of the issues.

℞ CHARTING YOUR RED FLAGS

At this point, be patient with yourself and the process. The chart we use as an illustration on the next page looks complicated in its fully completed form, but I hope you will find that it's fairly simple when you take it step-by-step. Please trust that the usefulness and power of the results really make the process worthwhile.

To help you visualize all that I just said, I'm using a couple who has identified contrasts on the following issues: extraversion, spirituality, personal order, risk taking, physical activity, enjoyment of the outdoors, and an argumentative nature. Let's look at how those issues might be explored with the aid of the chart. The gender signs ♀ (female) and ♂ (male) are used to mark where each individual is on the scale.

Here are the steps you take. Stop after each one and compare to the worksheet example:

1. **List the red flags**. On the chart entitled "Assessment of Red Flags," record in the Red Flag column all the possible mismatch items you have both identified.

2. **Mark the scale**. Plot on the percentile scale approximately where each of you ranks using the female symbol "♀" and the male symbol "♂" to identify which is which (So for example, if you're a "30" in tidiness and he is a "95" circle the "30" for you, the "95" for him, and mark it appropriately.)

3. **Determine the gap**. Calculate how far apart you are in each of

these areas. Take the two scores and subtract the lowest from the highest. (Continuing my example. The guy is a "95" on tidiness; the woman, a "30." (95-30=65). The number "65" represents their gap.)

4. **Rate the Importance**. Code the importance of each item on a 3-point scale:

   3 = vitally important, 2 = important, 1 = moderately important

5. **Multiply**. Next, multiply the importance score (1, 2, or 3) by each percentile gap (0 to 90).

6. **Amount of concern**. This yields the "amount of concern" this red flag represents: the larger the number, the greater the concern.

Assessment of Red Flags • Example Chart

Red Flag	Plotting the Percentile Scale Low　　　　High	Gap	X	Impor-tance	=	Amount of Concern
Extraversion	♂　♀ 10 20 30 40 50 60 70 80 90	(70 – 40) 30	X	2	=	60
Spirituality	♂　♀ 10 20 30 40 50 60 70 80 90	(90 – 70) 20	X	3	=	60
Personal order	♀　　　♂ 10 20 30 40 50 60 70 80 90	(90 – 30) 60	X	3	=	180
Risk taking	♀　　　♂ 10 20 30 40 50 60 70 80 90	(90 – 50) 40	X	2	=	80
Physically active	♀　　　♂ 10 20 30 40 50 60 70 80 90	(90 – 40) 50	X	3	=	150
Enjoys Outdoors	♀　♂ 10 20 30 40 50 60 70 80 90	(60 – 30) 30	X	1	=	30
Argumentative	♂　♀ 10 20 30 40 50 60 70 80 90	(70 – 40) 30	X	2	=	60

WHAT ARE THE IMPLICATIONS OF YOUR FINDINGS?

Since the conversations and exercises and arguments surrounding the issues that you have uncovered here will emerge from time to time throughout the course of your relationship, I want you to consider two guidelines for your conversations surrounding the red flags during the early stages of your relationship and up to just before marriage. One is the score showing "amount of concern" over a particular red flag, and the other is simply the number of red flags encountered.

℞ **Size of the score.** The bigger the "amount of concern" score, the greater the potential for damaging conflicts to arise. For this hypothetical couple, the big issues are "personal order" at 180 points, and "level of physical activity," at 150 points. Based on my experience in counseling, the other items that rate between 30 and 80 are probably quite resolvable with thoughtful attention. The two big ones on this chart (order and outdoors) may, upon careful scrutiny, prove to be disqualifiers. I know marriages where the discrepancy in personal order destroyed the relationship. I know others where a very physically active person married to a moderately active person created a relationship that could not survive. Whether the couple described on the chart can work out those differences is dependent entirely on their ability to adapt to each other. But, far better for them to consider this before they marry rather than after!

℞ **The number of red flags.** Four or five red flags are probably no problem since even successfully married couples experience between five and ten red flags of varying levels of seriousness. But if you have thirty red flags, you'll probably never find enough common ground between you to be comfortable, or you'll find that you have to work at the relationship so hard that the joy is sapped out of it.

YOUR TURN

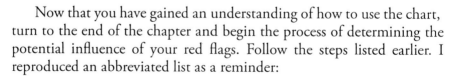

Now that you have gained an understanding of how to use the chart, turn to the end of the chapter and begin the process of determining the potential influence of your red flags. Follow the steps listed earlier. I reproduced an abbreviated list as a reminder:

1. **List the red flags.**

2. **Mark the scale** by circling the approximate percentile score for each of you.

3. **Determine the gap** by subtracting the highest number from the lowest.

4. **Rate the Importance** on a scale of: 3 = vitally important, 2 = important, 1 = moderately important.

5. **Multiply** the importance score by the percentile gap to determine the **level of concern**.

This is not a one-shot deal. During the course of your relationship you will encounter new issues. When this occurs, pull out the chart and consider the implications by going through the steps again.

THE MOST IMPORTANT POINT OF THE CHAPTER

I emphasize that you will always need to be aware of the mismatches as well as deal with risk factors due to external circumstances. That is why this exercise is so important. The more conversations you have around your similarities and differences the more likely it will be that you go into a relationship informed and prepared to face your red flags. You need to be prepared to either welcome your potential partner as he is, accepting that he may never change, or leave the relationship. In reality, if you're practicing good marriage-building techniques, it's very likely the gap will reduce in size, particularly if it's one of your own negative personal qualities that you are consciously working on to improve. However, the caution is, do not ever marry with the expectation that the gap will reduce. If you do that, you're marrying the "potential monster" I told you about in the introduction to "Step One: Take a Look Inward." Be willing to overcome the degree of difference as you discover it not after attempts to accommodate or change, which may or may not be lasting. I have found, too many times, that one or the other party in a relationship worked to change a negative behavior while they were dating just so that the marriage day could occur.

℞

While I have spent a good bit of time orienting to the idea, analysis, and conversations surrounding your red flags, as you can imagine, the sheer quantity of possible mismatches could fill an entire book. On the next few pages you will find five classic examples that we encounter frequently during our seminars and counseling sessions. They include mismatches due to differences in extraversion, energy, cultural background, socio-economic status, and intelligence.

CLASSIC EXAMPLES OF MISMATCHES

The following illustrations may give you further ideas of what you might personally experience, but more importantly they include conversations around how you might bridge the gap or determine if it is a disqualifier. As you begin to recognize how to deal with red flags in the examples presented, you will gain the understanding necessary to recognize and deal with others that you face.

Introversion versus Extraversion

Red flags, as I said, can also be personal qualities that are merely dissimilar, those you simply apply a "versus" to them. As an example, in my marriage I am the extravert and Darren is the introvert. Now, we knew this before we got married and we also knew that the gap was substantial, creating a red flag. Using the chart as well as an external test, we found that Darren was in the fortieth percentile in terms of extraversion and I was in the ninety-fifth, creating a fifty-five point difference. Because my gregarious nature is extremely central to my identity and his preference for solitude is fundamental for his research, we rated it a "3—vitally important." So using our chart we found we had a 165 point "amount of concern" (55 x 3 = 165). This represented one of three substantial red flags in our relationship. Prior to marriage, we discussed how this might influence our interaction. We understood that the introvert tends to wear down fairly quickly in a non-structured social setting. An extravert in the same setting tends to gain energy throughout the course of the evening. The pattern fit Darren and me perfectly. So in any given social setting by the time we'd been there for around two hours, Darren was ready to go home and sink into what I call his thinking cave—working on his research psychology and statistics and be inside that wonderful mind of his—and I was wanting to stay to the end of the party and then go to the "after party" if there was one.

If we had not considered how to respond to this red flag, some dysfunctional patterns would have emerged. Darren may have resisted going with me to attend a social function. I may have been upset when he was reluctant to stay for the full evening, thinking he didn't like my friends and community-service groups. But because we considered and dealt with the issue before we married, we experience essentially no conflict now. Here's how we did it:

Fundamentally, we accept that there will *always* be a difference in the way we approach a group setting. Because he is an introvert, I'm willing to protect him from too many meetings and too many social settings. He celebrates the fact that I enjoy people and that I gather my energy from people. He realizes that it is important for me to be able to express myself in a social setting so he never, ever takes that away from me. In fact, we have an easy solution that handles most situations. We simply take two cars so he can leave when he's had enough, and I can stay. When I want him to attend a particular social event, I first tell him why it's important to me. Then we strategize at what point in the evening it would be socially acceptable for him to excuse himself. He always comes, doesn't complain and participates with all the enthusiasm an introvert can muster. Our friends celebrate our "bridge technique" with us and laugh when the brainy caveman wants to return home, leaving his social butterfly to chat a while longer. We have created a win-win situation out of a red flag. We also laugh with each other over how absurdly different our perspectives are from time to time.

This example offers a wealth of information about the "mismatch" type of red flags:

- First of all it is a good model because it parallels the dynamics of many other red flags,

- It makes use of a percentile scale to identify how different the partners really are,

- It illustrates the importance of pre-awareness of the issue,

- It demonstrates acceptance of a foundational difference,

- And, it shows how resolution of the issue can nullify potential negative consequences.

Different Levels of Psychic Metabolism

The phrase, "psychic metabolism" is really just a fancy psychological phrase for "high energy" and "low energy." Just as there may be huge differences in the physical metabolism (that influences heart rate, caloric consumption, autonomic processes), there are differences in psychic metabolism.

A red flag is created when two people marry who are of different psychic metabolisms. This increases the likelihood of challenges to the relationship because the high-energy person is roused for immediate response, geared for action, and proceeds quickly and energetically to the accomplishment of whatever task is set before them. Meanwhile, the low-energy partner is of a more passive temperament; laid-back and low-key is part of their definition.

The low-energy category is epitomized by a lady I knew who would typically show up for church about ten minutes before the service was over. When she invited friends to after-church dinner, she would potter around the kitchen for three and a half hours for an eventual 4:30 p.m. luncheon. She was single and in her early forties, without a clear career path, having taken classes from time to time to complete an always in-progress two-year degree at the local junior college. She had never married, but since she was both attractive and social had been through a long string of boy friends initially attracted to her beauty, they eventually realized that they could not possibly handle her level of passivity.

If the difference of psychic metabolisms is relatively small it can actually enhance the marriage—if the couple allows themselves to be influenced by each other.[2] The high energy one can be calmed down a bit, and the partner with the slower psychic metabolism can be energized to take quicker action when appropriate. If the difference is extreme, however, a marriage would guarantee a continual feeling of irritation and discontent. The high-energy wife would be held back at every turn by her low-energy husband who, by contrast, would feel continually harassed and irritated by her unquenchable enthusiasm. People who are unaware of different psychic metabolisms typically feel an increasing sense of discomfort in the relationship but aren't quite sure why. Unfortunately many will marry before they figure it out.

But is it really possible that two such persons might be attracted to each other in the first place? The answer is a distressing "yes." Even the high-energy person requires times of shut down, periods of repose and non-tension. In those moments an attractive, enticing, opposite-sexed person of the profoundly low-key temperament might be balm to her harried life. The couple may even think they merely have opposite biorhythms, their pattern of physical, emotional and mental activity. The problem is that they may realize too late that while she is passive perhaps 15 percent of the time, her nurturing mate is 100 percent passive. Eighty-five percent of the time their lives will be plagued by a contrast so severe that interaction is barely possible. This is much like the "babbling brook" coupled with the "dead sea" example at the beginning of the chapter. In fact I have seen many couples attracted to opposite qualities—almost always with unhappy or disastrous results.

From Different Cultural Backgrounds

Even in our current culture of celebrating diversity, the fact remains that if two people marry who are of different cultural backgrounds, there is increased likelihood of challenges to the success of that relationship. While increasingly there are highly successful inter-ethnic marriages, one needs to look beneath the surface to understand *why* marriages made up by partners from different cultures might statistically be less successful. It becomes quickly apparent that the color of the skin and the facial features are not the critical factors. Researchers have found the problem: people from different cultures often exhibit dramatically different ways of thinking, perceiving, or responding to their worlds.[3] Let's use an example of two hypothetical individuals.

Recognizing that it is the cultural differences underlying the ethnicity that creates the challenges, let's consider the following contrasting example. David, a Caucasian living and going to university in Canada, applied to take a one-year student-mission trip after completing his third year as a religious-studies major. He was overjoyed to find that he was assigned to tropical Fiji and while there met one of the local girls. Lily was beautiful, charming, warm, encouraging, exotic and enticing. The two were soon in love and they married before the year was completed. Unfortunately, she had never traveled outside her own island environment. The following problems emerged over the next two years after the couple moved to Canada.

David had grown up loving snow and all the frosty winter activities that went with it and wanted to share that with Lily, but she was miserable during the months of arctic cold in the Canadian winter.

Lily's friends spent their high school years talking about being married and having children, focusing on a life centered on family and close relationships; David's closest high school buddies went to college, and he had goals to finish a master's degree and become a pastor.

Religion to Lily was merely a part of the gentle culture of her island, but she joined David's evangelical denomination, influenced totally by her desire to please her fiancé. He was driven by his goal to serve; she had never contemplated a life of sacrifice and commitment to others in the same life style or level as his.

Lily enjoyed a measured pace of life and wanted it to unfold in a known manner, consistent with her laid-back culture; David wanted to try new things and explore the world.

Unfortunately, with Lily and David, these underlying cultural differences tore them apart.

Different Socio-Economic Backgrounds

We acknowledge with a chuckle the consternation of a poor person if we were to suggest that marrying a rich person might be a problem. The penniless person contemplating such a situation might cry out with Tevya (in *Fiddler on the Roof* in response to Perchik's dictum that wealth is a curse), "God, if wealth be a curse, then strike me with it! . . . and may I never recover!"[4] But in the real world, the rich-poor marriage does indeed create problems.

Interestingly, the issue is not the absence or presence of money. It is the molding that has occurred throughout the life of each individual and the mindset that has resulted. Consider Patricia who grew up in wealth. Everything she ever wanted was there in abundance and if she didn't have it, mom's credit card took care of that in a hurry. Her family's home was spectacular; a Mercedes and Lexus graced the heated garage; she loved shopping and accumulated a lovely wardrobe and fixed up her room (canopied bed and chandeliers) just the way she liked it. Her wealthy parents rarely had time to cook so they typically ate out or had food ordered in. A maid was hired to keep the house clean, and upon graduation from high school she received a brand new Celica as a gift with the promise of "something nicer" when she finished college. So while she may have observed the work ethic and community-service contributions of her parents, her life was handed to her on a silver platter.

Let's contrast Patricia with Paul who grew up in poverty. Things Paul wanted were rarely provided except the basics of food, transportation, and second-hand clothing. There was no credit card, only the welfare check and food stamps. If Paul wanted anything of substance (say a bicycle) he would have to scrimp and save before he could acquire the second-hand version. Parked in the street in front of their depression era farmhouse was their 1987 Taurus, which ran occasionally. When it broke down (which was often) they could not afford a mechanic but had to try to get Uncle Harlow to figure out the problem. The bus or bicycle was frequently their only mode of transport. Paul essentially never shopped and his room was stark, functional, and shared by his younger brother. Eating out was a treat that rarely occurred more than once a year. Upon graduating from high school Paul was presented with a graduation card and five dollars to spend any way he liked.

Assuming that Paul and Patricia marry and have to actually make their own living, Patricia is ill equipped for survival. Few entry-level jobs provide the sort of income that supports her tastes and while Paul is used to restraint, careful planning, saving, and budgeting, Patricia isn't. A $2,500 splurge by Patricia on some fashionable clothing with matching accessories obliterates their budget for the next three years and drives poor Paul up the proverbial wall. These challenges ensure that a constant state of tension will pervade the marriage. If Patricia's parents are unintentionally foolish enough to bail them out after her splurges, the problem may be perpetual.

Do financial pressures provide challenges to a marriage? Absolutely! In fact, psychological research identifies financial discord as the greatest single issue that breaks relationships.[5] In the scenario presented above, the foundational differences are as extreme as the cultural differences described earlier, but there are myriad shades of gray that can trip you up. Once again, it's not about the absence or presence of money, but the molding and attitudes of a lifetime that create automatic friction.

Whether this problem can be solved depends primarily on the ability of the couple to appreciate each other's perspective. If Patricia's measure of Paul's love for her is based on his ability to provide as well as her parents, she has created an almost impossible barrier. Conversely, if she can learn to understand boundaries and appreciate that financial prosperity is a product of both healthy income *and* responsible expenditures, the relationship may manage necessary adjustments. Presence of wealth does not mean absence of responsibility. Absence of wealth does not mean a person is obligated to remain in poverty. The story of Paul is not random. It is the story (minus the 1987 Taurus and other minor details) of Henry Ford who eventually achieved astonishing levels of wealth. However, if the differences of wealth represent "foundational temperamental and personal differences," the relationship won't work. If you know you have this red flag but are not sure if it's a problem or not, allow a counselor to help you sort out whether this is a gap that can be bridged.

Intelligence

Remember the movie *IQ?* No amount of love (or deceit) could realistically bridge the gap between the main characters and the fact is, persons who marry who differ significantly in intelligence place their marriage at substantial risk.[6]

Let's use actual IQ points to illustrate. Since the average intelligence score is one hundred, 50 percent of people fall below that number and 50 percent above. A discrepancy of twenty to thirty points may be quite satisfactory *depending* on the importance of intelligence to a person's identity. In every day life, someone with an above average intelligence (say 115) married to a person who is somewhat below (say 90) may work fairly well *if* the IQ discrepancy does not significantly affect their daily actions. The 115 individual could probably do finances better and be more insightful in a number of settings. But if the couple match fairly well on their essences, share a wealth of enjoyed activities and love each other, perhaps acknowledging that one is a bit brighter than the other, the relationship can work. Research psychology, however would still list it as a red flag. Uncomfortable as it may seem to think about it, an IQ discrepancy spells challenges to the marriage.

A more extreme discrepancy suggests automatic ineligibility and should be listed as a disqualifier. Much like our character in the movie, consider the Ph.D. research chemist who loves her work and glories in a mind that is able to both comprehend and thrive in this very challenging discipline. Even an average Ph.D. chemist would likely have an IQ in the 150 – 170 range. If such a woman were to marry someone of average intelligence (IQ = 100), we are now talking a fifty to seventy point discrepancy. The one hundred-point person, no matter how much he wanted to, no matter how much he tried, no matter how much he read, no matter how much he studied, could never experience and appreciate his wife's world. Consider then how lonely life would be for the woman living with and married to a person who could never understand or participate in the things that are her life's work.

Up to this point in the chapter, we have been examining red flags that are due to mismatches in personal qualities. While the majority of your conversations will revolve around these, there are some outlying challenges that you may encounter that create additional risk factors. These are due to external factors that are beyond your control. The section below introduces some of the most common examples.

℞ Risk Factors that Arise from External Circumstance

This class of red flags simply exists as fact. For example, if your parents divorced, you automatically have this type of red flag. These flags are based on the external circumstances of your life. They are associated with conditions, personal practice, or factors external to the couple that puts their relationship at risk. Unfortunately, if you are facing one of these external circumstances, research shows you have an increased risk factor in your relationship and you should be aware that they are potentially damaging. Remember Walter and Amy in the biaser chapter and the disaster that turned out to be? They had an external circumstance—a long distance relationship—that increased their susceptibility to biasers.

Before I prompt you to make your list, let's look at three common external-circumstance red flags: a broken home, a long-distance relationship, and an unhappy extended family.

Broken Home

Research shows that those who come from a broken home, whether in their family of origin or their own previous relationship(s), are less likely to form successful marriages in the future.[7] Because the divorce rate has been high for many years, a lot of you are faced with this red flag, and it comes in two varieties: 1) two people seeking marriage for whom one or both have grown up in broken homes, and 2) individuals who have been divorced and are seeking remarriage. The example that follows applies to both circumstances although the dynamics of each situation is different. However, the two are closely related with the sad truth that, those who come out of a broken home are twice as likely to suffer divorce themselves.

The problem with a broken home (family of origin or divorce) and the reason why it is a red flag is that the participants have, in most instances, seldom seen a good marriage or a home that operates effectively. In other words they did not live within or view a good model. Observation of a friend's smoothly running marriage rarely provides an understanding of the dynamics of their friend's successful marriage or how they might do it themselves. Modeling has been shown to be one of the most powerful predictors of a wide array of behaviors, whether positive or negative. Examples: broken homes tend to produce broken homes; academic families tend to produce scholars; musical families often produce musicians; low socio-economic status families in many cases produce additional poverty. In the instance of a broken home or divorce, awareness of those things that went wrong does not necessarily provide an understanding of avenues for doing it right. In short, those who have never seen a good marriage are usually condemned to failure in their own marriages unless they get substantive help from people who have a clear understanding of the dynamics of how to overcome these internalized poor models.

R̥   *Long-Distance Relationship*

People are often, by nature or circumstances, forced to pursue a relationship at a distance. There are times in which distance does, indeed, "make the heart grow fonder." There are other times when the distance factor ends the relationship, weakens it, or disguises its true nature. There are, in fact, specific indicators to identify whether proximity will serve to bring you closer or will distance you.

Research, again shows that those who pursue a courting relationship at a distance are less likely to form a successful marriage than those who pursue a courtship together.[8] If you began a relationship in the same location but are continuing it apart, the less complete the knowledge of the two people prior to being separated, the greater the likelihood that the ensuing marriage will prove to be unsatisfactory.[9]

The primary difficulty with distance relationships is that it is quite possible to develop powerful emotions toward someone we know very poorly or not at all. Consider the teen infatuation for a movie star or other public figure. The emotion may be foolish or misplaced but there is no questioning its intensity. People who connect on the Internet find that they can develop an intense passionate love for each other even though they have never met. As we have already established, intense emotions blind. The same dynamic applies to someone with whom we have had brief contact. There is a greater awareness of the personal chemistry, but the importance of factual knowledge tends to slip into the background in the face of intense feelings of love.[10]

Whatever the startup method, it is quite possible for the emotions to continue to grow as the phone bill accelerates and the e-mails fly back and forth. The problem is that one begins to develop an image of the other so biased by their emotions that in time the image bears little resemblance to the reality. The idealized picture grows. It is rich in all the warm, nurturing, exciting, sexy qualities—the precise image depends on the needs of the individual—and is devoid of any negative qualities.

If you are pursuing a distance relationship please keep the list of biases handy and ask yourself daily, one by one, "Am I being blinded by this one?"

Unhappiness of Extended Family ℞

Those who have antagonistic relationships with in-laws, extended family, or close friends or associates are significantly less likely to be successful in their marriage.[11] As you can see, this concern potentially encompasses all close relationships. Because we are social beings, we crave the support and approval of significant others in our lives. When dating someone, given a fairly normal level of social awareness, it is keenly important that others appreciate the person we are dating and provide support. There are many individuals, whether young, naïve, or strongly independent, who despite absence of support from others choose to defy this principle. They feel that their love is enough to carry them through, no matter what others think. We recognize the following simplistic example because it is the way teenagers typically think: I like pizza, you like pizza; I like movies, you like movies; I hate my parents, you hate your parents; are we made for each other or what! Clearly, as one gets older the comparable items change, but these individual's disregard for others' opinions do not.

The desire and need for approval is first experienced when we are young, but it remains important in many relational circumstances. When Darren and I were dating he was living in Alberta; I was in Alabama. Several extended visits to Alabama, California (home of Darren's parents) and Alberta were negotiated during the courtship phase. We were concerned that while my family and friends met him a few times and his met me, nobody had a reasonable chance to really assess us together as a couple due to our distance relationship. As the years have gone by, we have had to actively work toward helping each other establish relationships with each others' friends and family of origin, knowing the importance of that support network.

There are enough challenges being met early in the marriage that when negativity is experienced from family members it may be the final straw. In contrast, during times of distress the support of important others can provide the stability necessary to smooth the road to continued relationship. Darren tells the story of a fellow doctoral student at UCLA to illustrate this point:

> When I first met Mojgan, who was Persian, she was single, but later married while still attending UCLA. We spoke often about customs in her culture. She told me that parents play an active role in the marriage-choice process. The parents don't choose for their children, but if a Persian woman is considering dating a

man (or vice versa) she discusses with her parents whether he might be a good marriage risk. The two families will then get together and discuss the viability of the relationship further. Once the marriage occurs, both extended families contribute unlimited support to the success of the newly married pair. The result? An extraordinarily low divorce rate of only one to two percent in the Persian culture.

The statistic alone is startling in this example, and I hope that you noticed that the families of the respective parities were doing much of what I have been asking you to do in the last couple of chapters. But, since we North Americans value our independence, even from our parents, we don't have that overt familial check in place. However, their approval or disapproval can tell us much about our choice in a mate, assuming they are able to judge from an objective standpoint. Therefore, when you are in a relationship, it is good to monitor together the reaction of your parents, family and close friends. If there is significant resistance to the individual you chose, or the idea of your marriage together, it is time for a careful assessment. If you have strong support from all sources, wonderful! However, realize that the greater the resistance, the greater the threat to the success of your marriage.

If you encounter resistance, consider the following:

1. Who is resisting? Is it someone who will have an ongoing impact on your relationship? How great will that impact be? The closer the resister is to you, and the greater the influence on the relationship, the greater the challenge will be to you and your partner's success.

2. Is the attitude likely to change? There are some instances in which you have extensive evidence that given a time of adjustment the antagonistic person will come around. While there is still the possibility that the two of you may not marry, the disapproving parent may express powerful concerns as long as the outcome is still being weighed in the balance. Once the marriage has occurred, then there are instances where they accept the reality and throw their support behind the success of the relationship. There are other instances, backed up by millions of case studies, where in-laws were, are, and will continue to be antagonistic. In that case, an ongoing relationship between the two of you and that antagonistic element will be a cancer in the marriage. The marriage may survive, but substantial heartache and damage is likely to accrue.

Creating Your Own List of External Circumstances

The above three examples obviously represent only a fraction of the external circumstances that can cause strife in a relationship. Other common risk-oriented red flags include: family of origin that was violent, destructive, beset with arguments; too short a courtship, and cohabitation prior to marriage.

At the end of the chapter I've included a worksheet that provides space to identify your "risk" circumstances as well as prompt conversation about how you will handle them and what type of individual you might speak to or work with to assist you in dealing with the issues. If you have any of the items mentioned above in your own life, be sure to include them.

CONCLUDING THOUGHTS

You need to take a deep look into yourself and be realistic about how much effort you're willing to put into marital health. If you know for sure or even suspect that you're not an enthusiastic relationship builder, then for you to have a successful relationship, there needs to be a smaller number of red flags without serious degrees of difference. On the other hand, take Darren and myself. We are willing to take on a few substantial red flags because we actually enjoy—even thrive on—relationship development. I have the confidence as well that Darren isn't intentionally irritating me as a disagreement occurs because of one of our mismatches. This recognition about "intentionality" is huge to the health of a relationship. When you recognize that the annoying thing that your partner does arises out of a red flag, that it is not meant to intentionally prod, poke or even hurt you, then the rift is lessened. Because you can recognize that the attitude or action is not intentional it helps, daily, to reduce your degree of emotional response and act more rationally.

What Darren and I have discovered is that because we know our mismatches are not disqualifiers, we can commit to bridge any abyss. Once we understand that what we are facing is a red flag then we are able to overcome the mismatch because we believe that our relationship is well worth the work.

List of Red Flags Her List	
Name:	
1.	
2.	
3.	
4.	
5.	
6.	
7.	
8.	
9.	
10.	

List of Red Flags His List	
Name:	
1.	
2.	
3.	
4.	
5.	
6.	
7.	
8.	
9.	
10.	

Assessment of Red Flags

Her name: _____ His name: _____

Red Flag	Plotting the Percentile Scale Low High	Gap	X	Impor-tance	=	Amount of Concern
	10 20 30 40 50 60 70 80 90		X		=	
	10 20 30 40 50 60 70 80 90		X		=	
	10 20 30 40 50 60 70 80 90		X		=	
	10 20 30 40 50 60 70 80 90		X		=	
	10 20 30 40 50 60 70 80 90		X		=	
	10 20 30 40 50 60 70 80 90		X		=	
	10 20 30 40 50 60 70 80 90		X		=	
	10 20 30 40 50 60 70 80 90		X		=	
	10 20 30 40 50 60 70 80 90		X		=	
	10 20 30 40 50 60 70 80 90		X		=	
	10 20 30 40 50 60 70 80 90		X		=	

Note: A full size chart is available for free download in your Bonus at: www.TheCompatibilityCode.com/bonus

Red Flags Due to External Circumstances

Circumstance:

Ideas for handling the negative aspects of this circumstance:

People to assist you:

Circumstance:

Ideas for handling the negative aspects of this circumstance:

People to assist you:

Circumstance:

Ideas for handling the negative aspects of this circumstance:

People to assist you:

* Chapter 12 *

CREATING FOREVER ENDINGS

Stories that Have Wonderful Beginnings *and* Endings

W̶e never skip a final chapter in a murder mystery, but I think we often skim or omit the last chapter in books where we sense that the material is merely a summation. If I could have put this chapter first, I would have. It's that momentous because it covers the two most important factors of a successful marriage. But, you can't put the cart before the horse and still get the job done, so while this chapter is about beginnings it comes last because it's also about forever endings. As my gift to you, it's an entire bag of pixie-dust for you to sprinkle over your precious new relationship. Because of all the work you've done, you have studied in the right library and are hunting in the right forest. You have a list that keeps you focused and determination to stay the course. Maybe by now, you are in a relationship where love is blossoming; maybe you're about to get married and you're transitioning from "finding" to "keeping." There's actually one more element to the compatibility code that you need to apply, however. It's about how to turn a new beginning into a forever ending.

℞ THE GIVE-GIVE RELATIONSHIP

Forever endings have two components or success factors. The first is the give-give relationship, which truly creates a platform for a marvelous relationship experience. Observe how it works. The husband recognizes that his wife thinks differently and has different needs than his own. Because of this, he spends lavish amounts of time to learn to know his wife, to understand her, to find what brings her pleasure, what lights her fire, what tickles her fancy, what nurtures her soul. As his understanding increases he delights in giving to his wife in the way that brings her pleasure.

The wife also recognizes that her husband's needs and thought processes are different than hers. She takes copious amounts of time discovering what refreshes his spirit, what brings him happiness, what scratches his itch, what satisfies his hungers. Then as understanding increases, she is able to give to her beloved in ways that are pleasing to him. This provides the relationship with amazing power. It keeps the couple from becoming complacent as they're always searching for ways to give, and it helps to keep the relationship "fresh" in those monotonous times when it can get stale. If our ultimate goal is to grow a marriage, the give-give relationship is the water that you pour over your relationship everyday so that it blossoms into the greatness of real love. Without it, however, your love may wither and die.

In celebration of the give-give relationship that Darren and I share, he wrote this chapter as a surprise for me, a gift I could in turn share with you. The idea of the give-give relationship actually comes from legendary UCLA psychologist, Harold Kelley, who spent much of his career researching human relationships. To illustrate even very complex phenomena he would often revert to a two-by-two matrix to illustrate his points. On the issue of marital success, Kelley constructed a two-by-two diagram that characterizes four different types of marriage based on whether each partner is "a giver," one who is altruistic and caring for the needs of others, or "a taker," one who is fundamentally selfish and self-absorbed.[1] He identifies the giver by the lower- or upper-case letter G and the taker by the lower- or upper-case letter T. The placement of these letters is illustrated on one of Kelley's diagrams on the next page.

		MAN	
		G (giver)	**T** (taker)
W O M A N	**g** (giver)	**ABUNDANCE** (G – g)	**TORMENT** (T – g)
	t (taker)	**TORMENT** (G - t)	**ESCAPE** (T - t)

Notice that the four sections of the diagram are labeled as follows:

- **Abundance:**   **G – g**   (man is a Giver, woman is a giver)
- **Torment:**   **T – g**   (man is a Taker, woman is a giver)
- **Torment:**   **G – t**   (man is a Giver, woman is a taker)
- **Escape:**   **T – t**   (man is a Taker, woman is a taker)

As you can guess, the Escape or "T-t" relationship is the most negative. Those who reside there are usually quite unhappy. The possibility of two selfish and self-absorbed people surviving a marriage is very low indeed. Successful marriages involve a lifetime of studying and giving to each other—something for which selfish people have little skill. The only fortune of the Escape relationship is that the disaster is so evident that the relationship usually ends quickly.

The Torment categories with the "G-t" or the "T-g" type combination are probably the most painful. Here we have one person who enjoys giving and caring and a partner who enjoys taking. While initially this may sound like a wonderfully complementary match—for example, someone who is a great listener marrying someone who talks all the time—the opposite is actually true. This type of relationship produces perpetual torment, particularly for the giver. Unlike the "Escape" relationship that breaks quickly, the "Tormented" relationships often work for a while. The giver takes pleasure in giving and the taker takes pleasure in being given to. However, sooner or later, the giver begins to feel taken advantage of. There is a simple reason for this. He or she *is* being taken advantage of. While the giver continues to give she does not receive what is necessary for her own revitalization. The torment grows slowly as the giver progressively hopes that, by more giving, the taker will begin to reciprocate. Occasionally they do, but usually not. Such a marriage eventually grows into a loveless prison. Sometimes divorce provides a pardon, but many times the marriage stays together in a brooding, seething, lethal quietness that singes the spirit of anyone who enters and deadens the lives of those who are the unlucky participants.

So how and why does the give-give relationship create abundance and work so well? All people have needs in the context of a relationship: the need to be heard, to be understood, to be nurtured, to be cared for, to be loved. To understand this further, we measure doses of these qualities with what we might call Need Fulfillment (NF) points—sort of like the "recommended daily allowance" (RDA) of vitamins and minerals in food. Let's say a particular person requires fifteen NF points to fulfill her RDA of love. As long as she gets her fifteen NF points a day she's fine. But if she receives fewer than the fifteen points a day, her love tank begins to empty and suffering results. The exciting news is that those who follow the pattern of the give-give relationship, with their extraordinary efforts to understand and give to the other, are typically providing fifty or sixty NF points per day and live in abundance. As long as the nurturing support each is receiving is so much greater than their needs, then when the inevitable day comes when neither provides each other any NF points, both partner's love tanks are so full that the occasional challenges are easily weathered. This applies just as wonderfully to the occasional squabble or disappointment. So the lesson is this: those who go into a marriage (or a dating relationship) with this perspective of give-give and reasonable compatibility will experience a relationship that thrives. In some ways it's that simple; a mutual decision to give to one another. In other ways it's so complicated that it could fill a book. In a previous marriage, I was often a "taker" and looking back, I could see that he was more often a "giver." And although other things were the final cause of our divorce, years later I have been able to see that by being a "taker," I created torment in our marital atmosphere.

Thankfully, giving to one another is a conscious choice. Darren and I choose to create a relationship based on the give-give principles, with amazing results. We know if we present needs to one another, they will be met. Darren, speaking to me in a soft voice full of warmth, says that in our give-give relationship he feels "lavished upon and secure and satisfied and loved." Indeed, that is an important part of "happily ever after."

The second component is not only what we have or feel together, it is what we *do* together.

SHARED PURPOSE

℞

In previous chapters we have frequently emphasized that matching of essence qualities is the single most important factor in determining compatibility. Future success in marriage is dependent not only on the foundation of compatibility but also on a powerful idea that arises out of matched essences. The marriages that are really exceptional typically have a shared purpose, more accurately a *passionate* shared purpose.

As we've talked with couples who share excellent marriages, it is apparent that while a strongly matched set of essence qualities drew them together, they had taken that sharing one step further. They had identified not only how they were going to blend their interests together, but also how they were going to apply them jointly in their relationship and externally to others. Conversely, a serious mismatch of essence qualities typically defeats a couple's ability to find shared purpose because there is so little overlap of individual definition and interests. Because Darren and I have five amazingly matched essences, we also found several shared purposes. As our dating conversations progressed it became obvious that by far the most compelling was the desire to shift the perspective on how people meet and marry in such a way that it will have a positive influence on the success rate of marriages in North America.

We were fortunate in that we were able to verbalize this shared purpose early on. Observe our statement of that goal, quoted from an e-mail letter Darren wrote to me more than eight years ago while we were dating:

> You and I have already highlighted the areas of service to Him that we feel called into . . . such as leading a life of marital compatibility that prepares us to jointly write a book that He could use to reach others, to open our home to young people who are on the threshold of such critical life decisions, and be a vessel for Him to show His plan for marriage and family…

This sense of shared mission has guided much of our behavior during our marriage and is the impetus for this book, our first published material on the topic. More will follow, as this has become our lifework. As you know from spending time with me in the book, we conduct seminars and maintain an open home in which many feel comfortable.

As you can imagine, ideas about our shared purpose occupies many of our conversations and the material has become etched into our minds. Due to our enthusiasm for the subject and willingness to share it with others, people in need seek us out for assistance and counsel and we find that—and this is perhaps our greatest honor—we have been given the trust of others.

The subject of our shared purpose also assists in a number of practical ways in our own marriage. We feel that we have no right presenting this material if we do not, ourselves, have an excellent marriage. So the elements we present in this book we also practice in our own marriage. When we have a disagreement we often remind ourselves of our shared passion. We'll be in the middle of an argument (okay, I should be honest; I argue and Darren is patient), and one of us will stop and ask: "Do you think anyone else has experienced a problem similar to what we are facing right now?" Even if we are really upset or the problem is a daunting one, we know that similar issues have been faced by millions of people over the years. It instantly (usually) alters our focus away from the emotions of our distress and toward determining how to resolve this in a fashion that will better equip us to assist others in the future. We realize without saying it that, if we are unable to resolve the issue, our ability to help others or to maintain our credibility as marital experts is compromised.

At the end of the day, you can do the work I've outlined for you in this book. You can identify your disqualifiers and red flags. You most certainly should match your essences, but know that it takes a mutual awareness of shared purpose and both of you subscribing to a give-give attitude for your relationship to truly flourish. I think of the absence of these two aspects as the ultimate disqualifiers. If you don't have some sort of shared passion and you're not both willing to engage in a give-give relationship, then you should have serious thoughts about not getting married.

I don't want your heart to suffer any more. I believe in love and marriage and all the richness that it offers to us as human beings. That's the bottom line. It's the primary reason why I wrote this book. I want you to find your romance of the century. I want you to find the exquisite joy that comes from a marriage that is based on shared purposes, one that exhibits a matching of essences, one that thrives on the nectar of give-give.

 So to celebrate marriage I am leaving you, not with any last bits of advice, but with snapshots of love. To all of us looking in on them, they are wonderful examples of couples whose shared passion and purpose made them some of the most romantic and successful marriages through the centuries.

♥ There is Will and Ariel Durant, the creators of the ten-volume *History of Civilization*. During their sixty-six-year marriage, their love was always evident as they, together, created one of the most celebrated histories ever written. They died within two weeks of each other.

♥ Billy and Ruth Graham were married sixty-four years until Ruth's death in 2007. Billy without doubt was the most famous evangelist in modern history and was supported in his ministry with passion, zeal, and love by his wife throughout their life.

♥ While many have heard of Marie Curie as a pioneer in the field of radioactivity, it was both she and her husband Pierre Curie who worked together on their Nobel prize winning work in physics and chemistry. Talk about a legacy; not only did the couple receive the honor together, but Marie was awarded the prize a second time after Pierre's death and their child Irène and *her* husband were presented with a third Nobel prize. Although Marie and Pierre were already famous when they married, their productivity was far greater when they worked together and their love for each other is legendary.

♥ Love sometimes is strong but short-lived. Consider the tragically brief marriage of C.S. Lewis and Joy Gresham Lewis (depicted in the 1993 film *Shadowlands*, one of our popcorn night favorites). Despite Joy's illness, she worked with her husband on what he considered his best novel, *Till We Have Faces*.

♥ For you musicians, consider the extraordinarily productive life of legendary composer Robert Schumann and his wife Clara. Clips from their biography provide a glimpse:

On the day after their wedding Robert gave a diary to Clara for her birthday, suggesting that they each write and exchange the diary weekly. They continued this diary for several years. Today it serves as an intimate narrative of the lives of the two artists and the love affair of the century. Clara and Robert went on to a musical life together; she primarily as a concert pianist and he as a composer. Robert encouraged Clara to compose (Clara composed sixty-six works during her career, but a woman composer was not acknowledged in the mid 19th century); he secretly published the songs that she wrote during the first year of their marriage and then presented them to Clara on their first anniversary. Their musical interaction was intense, as they studied symphony scores together, shared reactions to performances, and read similar literature.

Robert died tragically young at forty-six; Clara lived another forty years and pursued a concert career to support her family. She became a superstar of her era. Her musical genius on the piano was considered by many to be equal or superior to that of Franz Liszt! She maintained a close friendship with Johannes Brahms during the final years of her life, but her deathbed wish tells us everything we need to know. She had her grandson play her husband's *F-sharp major Romance*. It was the last music Clara Schumann heard.[2]

♥   Finally, there is the marriage of British poets Robert Browning and Elizabeth Barrett Browning. When they married in 1846, both were already famous. Elizabeth had always been of fragile health but with marriage to Robert (and a move to Italy) her health improved dramatically and they lived a life of a shared passion of touching the lives of others through the beauty of poetry. Elizabeth's best-known poem contains one of the most famous opening lines in the English language. It is Sonnet #43 from *Sonnets from the Portuguese*.[3]

We conclude our book with this poem expressing Elizabeth's love to her husband. I cannot think of a more fitting end, for it expresses beautifully, as only poetry can, all that I've attempted throughout this book to make possible for you to experience:

How do I love thee? Let me count the ways.
I love thee to the depth and breadth and height
My soul can reach, when feeling out of sight
For the ends of Being and ideal Grace.
I love thee to the level of everyday's
Most quiet need, by sun and candle-light.
I love thee freely, as men strive for Right;
I love thee purely, as they turn from Praise.
I love thee with the passion put to use
In my old griefs, and with my childhood's faith.
I love thee with a love I seemed to lose
With my lost saints,—I love thee with the breath,
Smiles, tears, of all my life!—and, if God choose,
I shall but love thee better after death.[4]

♥ ♥ ♥ ♥ ♥

To the poetry of your new love. May it, too, last a life time and beyond.

Elizabeth and Darren George

NOTES

CHAPTER 1

1. MCA Records (Publisher). (1993). *American graffiti*. (CD Recording No. B000002081). Universal City, CA: MCA Records.
2. MCA Records (Publisher). (1993). *American graffiti*. (CD Recording No. B000002081). Universal City, CA: MCA Records.
3. Chapman, G. (2004). *The five love languages*. Chicago: Northfield Publishing.
4. Simpson, J. A., Campbell, B., Berscheid, E. (1986). The association between romantic love and marriage: Kephart (1967) twice revisited. *Personality and Social Psychology Bulletin, 12,* 363-372.
5. Cherlin, A. (1983). The trends: marriage, divorce, remarriage. In A.S. Skolnick and J.H. Skolnick (eds.), *Family in Transition* (4th edition, pp. 128-137). Boston: Little Brown.
5. Fine, M. A., & Fine, D. R. (1992). Recent changes in laws effecting stepfamilies: Suggestions for legal reform. *Family Relations, 41,* 334-340.
6. Popcak, G. (2002). *The exceptional seven percent*. New York: Citadel.
7. Felder, R. (2002). *Comments on celebrity marriages*. Retrieved March 13, 2008, from http://2000magazine.com/websightsone/jessenash/pages/jessedivorce.html.
8. MCA Records (Publisher). (1993). *American graffiti*. (CD Recording No. B000002081). Universal City, CA: MCA Records.
9. Snyder, M. (1987). *Public appearance/private realities: The psychology of self monitoring*. New York: W. H. Freeman.
10. Dobson, J. (2003). *Emotions can you trust them?* Englewood Cliffs, NJ: Regal Books.
11. Chapman, G. (2004). *The five love languages*. Chicago: Northfield Publishing.
12. Grover, K. J., Russell, C.S., Schumm, W. R., & Paff-Bergen, L. A. (1985). Mate selection processes and marital satisfaction. Family Relations, 34, 383-386.
13. Huston, T. L., Surra, C. A., Fitzgerald, N. M., & Cate, R. M. (1981). From courtship to marriage: Mate selection as an interpersonal process. In S. Duck & R. Gilmour (Eds.). *Personal relationships: Vol. 2. Developing personal relationships* (pp. 53-99). London: Academic.
14. Arista Records (Publisher). (2004). *Reflections: Carly Simon's greatest hits*. (CD Recording No. B001XANAS). New York: Arista Records.
15. Teti, D. M., Lamb, M. E., & Elster, A. B. (1987). Long-range economic and marital consequences of adolescent marriage in three cohorts of adult males. *Journal of Marriage and the Family, 49,* 499-506.

Chapter 2

1. Popcak, G. (2002). *The exceptional seven percent.* New York: Citadel.
2. Branden, N. (1985). *Honoring the self: Self esteem and personal transformation.* New York: Bantam.
3. Surra, C. A., & Longstreth, M. (1990). Similarity of outcomes, interdependence and conflict in dating relationships. *Journal of Personality and Social Psychology, 59,* 501-516.
4. Tennov, D. (1999). *Love and limerence: the experience of being in love.* New York: Scarborough House.
5. Fromm, E. (1955/2000). *The art of loving.* Centennial, CO: Centennial.
6. Gottman, J. M., & Silver, N. (1999). *The seven principles for making marriage work.* New York: Three Rivers Press.
7. Keillor, G. K. (Host, Producer). (airdate unknown). *A Prairie Home Companion.* American Public Media.

Chapter 3

1. Maslin, J. (December 23, 1994). *IQ (1994): How love is an art and not a science.* New York: New York Times Review. Retrieved March 11, 2008 from http://movies.nytimes.com/movie/review?res=980-DE5DF1F38F930A15751C1A962958260
2. Sternberg, R. J. (1986). A triangular theory of love. *Psychological Review, 93,* 119-135.
3. Infatuation. Retrieved March 11, 2008, from http://en.wikipedia.org/wiki/Infatuation.
4. Huston, T. L., Surra, C. A., Fitzgerald, N. M., & Cate, R. M. (1981). From courtship to marriage: Mate selection as an interpersonal process. In S. Duck & R. Gilmour (Eds.). *Personal relationships: Vol. 2. Developing personal relationships* (pp. 53-99). London: Academic.
5. Chapman, G. (2004). *The five love languages.* Chicago: Northfield Publishing.
6. Fromm, E. (1955/2000). *The art of loving.* Centennial, CO: Centennial.
7. Detweiler, M. C., & Hupp, S. M. (Eds.). (2001) *1001 ways to say I love you.* Grand Rapids, MI: Zondervan.
8. Chapman, G. (2004). *The five love languages.* Chicago: Northfield Publishing.

Chapter 4

1. Ulrich, R. E., Hutchinson, R.R., & Azrin, N.H. (1965). Pain-elicited aggression. *Psychological Record, 15,* 111-126.
2. Lewis, C. S. (1955/1998). *Surprised by joy* (p. 145). London: Fount.
3. Maslow, A. H. (1968). *Toward a psychology of being.* New York: D. Van Nostrand.
4. Soukhanov, A. H., & Rooney, K. (Eds.) (2004). Jealousy. *Encarta Webster's dictionary of the English language, 2nd edition.* New York: Bloomsbury.
5. John, E. (1984). *Who wears these shoes?* UK: Big Pig Music Limited.
6. Schulz, C. M. *Peanuts.* Retrieved on April 2, 2008 from http://www.quotesandpoem.com/quotes/showquotes/author/charles-m.-schulz/21857
7. Skinner, B. F. (1969). *Contingencies of reinforcement: A theoretical analysis.* New York: Appleton-Century-Crofts.
8. Rogers, C. R. (1961). *On Becoming a Person.* Boston: Houghton Mifflin.

CHAPTER 5

1.   Covey, S. (1997). *The seven habits of highly effective people*. New York: Golden Books.
2.   Rogers, C. R. (1951). *Client-centered therapy: Its current practice, implications, and theory*. Boston: Houghton Mifflin.
3.   Keillor, G. K. (1987). From Keillor's radio show *A Prairie Home Companion*, quoted in *The New York Times*, February 18, 1987.
4.   Taylor, S. E. (1989). *Positive illusions*. Jackson, TN: Basic Books Inc.
5.   Noble, A., & Hogg, P. S. (Eds.). (2001). *The Canongate Burns: The complete poems and songs of Robert Burns*. Edinburgh: Canongate.
6.   Anderson, N. H. (1968). Likableness ratings of 555 personality-trait words. *Journal of Social Psychology, 9,* 272-279.
7.   Shakespeare, W. (1599/1952). Much ado about nothing. In R. M. Hutchins (Ed.) *Great books of the western world*, (Vol. 26, p. 503). London: Encyclopaedia Britannica.

CHAPTER 6

1.   Erikson, E. H. (1968). *Identity, youth and crisis*. New York: Norton.
2.   Goodwin, D. K. (2005). The master of the game. In A. S. Moore (Ed.) *Time* (July 4, 2005, p. 49). New York: Time Inc.
3.   Goodwin, D. K. (2005). The master of the game. In A. S. Moore (Ed.) *Time* (July 4, 2005, pp. 49-50). New York: Time Inc.
4.   Goodwin, D. K. (2005). The master of the game. In A. S. Moore (Ed.) *Time* (July 4, 2005, p. 50). New York: Time Inc.
5.   Goodwin, D. K. (2005). The master of the game. In A. S. Moore (Ed.) *Time* (July 4, 2005, p. 50). New York: Time Inc.
6.   Goodwin, D. K. (2005). The master of the game. In A. S. Moore (Ed.) *Time* (July 4, 2005, p. 53). New York: Time Inc.
7.   Goodwin, D. K. (2005). The master of the game. In A. S. Moore (Ed.) *Time* (July 4, 2005, p. 54). New York: Time Inc.
8.   Goodwin, D. K. (2005). The master of the game. In A. S. Moore (Ed.) *Time* (July 4, 2005, p. 54). New York: Time Inc.
9.   Goodwin, D. K. (2005). The master of the game. In A. S. Moore (Ed.) *Time* (July 4, 2005, p. 54). New York: Time Inc.
10. Joel, B. (1977). *Just the way you are* from the album *The strangers*. Retrieved March 19, 2008 from http://www.lyrics007.com/BillyJoelLyrics/JustTheWayYouAreLyrics.html

CHAPTER 7

1.   Maltz, M. (1969). *Psycho-Cybernetics*. New York: Pocket Books.

CHAPTER 8

1.   Smith, T. W., & Gallo, L. C. (1999). Hostility and cardiovascular reactivity during marital interaction. *Psychosomatic Medicine, 61,* 436-445.
2.   Guerin, P. J. (1987). *The evaluation and treatment of marital conflict*. New York: Basic Books.
3.   Gottman, J. M., & Silver, N. (1999). *The seven principles for making marriage work*. New York: Three Rivers Press.
4.   Gottman, J. M., & Silver, N. (1999). *The seven principles for making marriage work*. New York: Three Rivers Press.
5.   Gottman, J. M., & Silver, N. (1999). *The seven principles for making marriage work*. New York: Three Rivers Press.

204 • The Compatibility Code

6. Luckey, E. B. (1964). Marital satisfaction and personality correlates of spouse. *Journal of Marriage and the Family, 26,* 217-220.
7. Haley, J. (1976). *Problem-solving therapy.* San Francisco: Jossey-Bass.
8. Spitzer, R. L., Gibbon, M., Skodol, A. E., Williams, J. B., & First, M. B. (2005). *DSM-IV Casebook.* Washington, DC: American Psychiatric Press.
9. James, R. K. (2005). *Crisis intervention strategies.* Belmont, CA: Brooks/Cole.
10. Gottman, J. M. (2001). *The relationship cure: A five-step guide for building connections with family, friends, and lovers.* New York: Three Rivers Press.
11. Popcak, G. (2002). *The exceptional seven percent.* New York: Citadel.
12. Bowen, M. (1976). Principles and techniques of multiple family therapy. In P. J. Guerin (Ed.), *Family therapy: Theory and practice.* New York: Gardner Press.
13. Spitzer, R. L., Gibbon, M., Skodol, A. E., Williams, J. B., & First, M. B. (2005). *DSM-IV Casebook.* Washington, DC: American Psychiatric Press.
14. Popcak, G. (2002). *The exceptional seven percent.* New York: Citadel.
15. Hazen, C., & Shaver, P. (1987). Romantic love conceptualized as an attachment process. *Journal of Personality and Social Psychology, 52,* 511-524.
16. Spitzer, R. L., Gibbon, M., Skodol, A. E., Williams, J. B., & First, M. B. (2005). *DSM-IV Casebook.* Washington, DC: American Psychiatric Press.
17. Gottman, J. M., & Silver, N. (1999). *The seven principles for making marriage work.* New York: Three Rivers Press.
18. Hooley, J. M., & Teasdale, J. D. (1989). Predictors of relapse in unipolar depressives: expressed emotion, marital distress and perceived criticism. *Journal of Abnormal Psychology, 98*(3), 229-235.
18. Gottman, J. M., & Silver, N. (1999). *The seven principles for making marriage work.* New York: Three Rivers Press.
19. Spitzer, R. L., Gibbon, M., Skodol, A. E., Williams, J. B., & First, M. B. (2005). *DSM-IV Casebook.* Washington, DC: American Psychiatric Press.
20. Myers, I. B. (2006). *Myers-Briggs Type Indicator Manual.* Mount Horeb, WI: Personality Development & Type Dynamics.
21. Cattell, R. B., Eber, H. W., & Tatsuoka, M. M. (1970). *Hand book of the 16 personality factor questionnaire.* Champaign, IL: Institute for Personality and Ability Testing.
22. Taylor, R. M. & Morrison, L. P. (2008). *Taylor-Johnson Temperament Analysis.* Simi Valley, CA: Psychological Publications.

Chapter 9

1. Homer, (c 700 B.C./1952). *The odyssey.* London: Encyclopaedia Britannica.
2. Getchell, R. (Producer), & Scorsese, M. (Director). (1974). *Alice Doesn't Live Here Any More* [Motion picture]. United States: Warner Home Video.
3. Huston, T. L., Surra, C. A., Fitzgerald, N. M., & Cate, R. M. (1981). From courtship to marriage: Mate selection as an interpersonal process. In S. Duck & R. Gilmour (Eds.). *Personal relationships: Vol. 2. Developing personal relationships* (pp. 53-99). London: Academic.
4. Spitz, R. A. (1946). Hospitalism: An inquiry into the genesis of psychotic conditions in early childhood. In *Psychoanalytic Study of the Child,* (Vol. 2). New York: International Universities Press.
5. Perlman, D., & Peplau, L. A. (1998). Loneliness. *Encyclopedia of Mental Health* (Vol. 2, pp. 571-581). New York: Academic Press.
6. Weiss, R. S. (1973). *Loneliness: The experience of emotional and social isolation.* Cambridge, MA: MIT Press.

7. Calvert, J. D. (1988). Physical attractiveness: A review and reevaluation of its role in social skill research. *Behavioral Assessment, 10,* 29-42.

8. *Statistical Abstract of the United States,* 1998 (p. 58) by U.S. Bureau of the Census, 1995, Washington, DC: U.S. Government Printing Office.

9. Nightingale, E. (1986). *Lead the field.* Chicago: Nightingale Conant.

10. Logue, A. W. (1995). *Self-Control: Waiting until tomorrow for what you want today.* Upper Saddle River, NJ: Prentice Hall.

CHAPTER 11

1. Chapman, G. (2004). *The five love languages* (pp. 71-73). Chicago: Northfield Publishing.

2. Gottman, J. M., & Silver, N. (1999). *The seven principles for making marriage work.* New York: Three Rivers Press.

3. Corey, G., & Corey, M. S. (2002). *Groups: Process and practice.* Pacific Grove, CA: Brooks/Cole.

4. Coe, F., & Prince, H. (Producers), & Jewison, N. (Director). (1971). *Fiddler on the roof* [Motion picture]. United States: MGM.

5. Brotherson, S. E. (2003). Time, sex, and money: challenges in early marriage. *Meridian Magazine.* Retrieved March 25, 2008 from http://www.meridianmagazine. com/familyconnections/030508marriagechallenges.html

6. Smith, M. (1941). Similarities of Marriage Partners in Intelligence. *American Sociological Review,* 6, 697-701.

7. Nock, S. L., & Brinig, M. F. (1999). *Divorce and the division of labor.* In The Edmonton Journal, November 29, 1999.

8. Brehm, S. S., Miller, R., Perlman, D., & Campbell, S. M. (2001). *Intimate Relationships.* New York: McGraw Hill.

9. Brehm, S. S., Miller, R., Perlman, D., & Campbell, S. M. (2001). *Intimate Relationships.* New York: McGraw Hill.

10. Ben Ze'ev, A. (2004). *Love online: emotions on the internet.* Cambridge: Cambridge University Press.

11. Brehm, S. S., Miller, R., Perlman, D., & Campbell, S. M. (2001). *Intimate Relationships.* New York: McGraw Hill.

CHAPTER 12

1. Kelley, H. H., & Thebaut, J. W. (1978). *Interpersonal relationships: A theory of interdependence.* New York: John Wiley & Sons.

2. Traxler, C. (1999). Clara Schumann. *Quarter Notes* (March, 1999). Retrieved on March 27, 2008 from http://www.geocities.com/Vienna/Strasse/1945/WSB/ clara.html

3. Blake, K. (1991). *The Relationship of Elizabeth Barrett Browning and Robert Browning.* Retrieved March 27, 2008 from http://www.victorianweb.org/authors/ebb/ebbio1.html

4. Browning, E. B. (1846). How do I love thee, let me count the ways. Retrieved May 14, 2008 from http://rpo.library.utoronto.ca/poem/3566.html

Icon Index

Prescripts, References, and Tools

by Chapter

Chapter 2: The Ideal Marriage

Prescripts: ℞

References: 📖

· ·

CHAPTER 3: WHAT'S LOVE GOT TO DO WITH IT?

PRESCRIPTS: ℞

REFERENCES: 📖

· ·

CHAPTER 4: EMOTIONAL GERMS

PRESCRIPTS: ℞

REFERENCES:

. . . .

CHAPTER 5: THE STRAIGHT TRUTH ABOUT SELF

PRESCRIPTS: ℞

REFERENCES:

TOOLS:

. . . .

· ·

CHAPTER 9: BIASERS: LURE OF THE SIRENS

· ·

* *

Chapter 10: Matching Essence Qualities

Prescripts: ℞

Tools: 🛠

* *

Chapter 11: Red Flags

Prescripts: ℞

CHAPTER 12: CREATING FOREVER ENDINGS

ABOUT THE AUTHORS
Elizabeth E. George, M.A.
AND Darren M. George, Ph.D.

How is it possible for an award-winning businesswoman and world class athlete like Elizabeth George to have been so unsuccessful in her first two attempts at marriage?

Consider her accomplishments:

- Selection as a "Top 40 Business Executive Under the Age of 40"
- CEO, Pre*fix* Solutions Inc., helping people act on professional and personal goals
- Economic development and tourism consultant
- University professor, Master's degree in Human Resource Management
- Christian lay counselor
- Mother of two beautiful young daughters
- World Champion in Crossbow, 5 time member U.S. International Shooting Team

To top it off, she even received the United States Government's coveted Distinguished International Shooter Badge, its highest award for marksmanship. So how could she have so badly missed the mark when it came to love?

She failed in love because she fell in love with the wrong men for the wrong reasons. That discovery was the turning point in her life, the end of false choices that left her lonely, and the beginning of a forever marriage to husband and co-author Darren George.

Darren George was a single parent too, in his case of teenage children, and he shared a resume as bright and internationally competitive as his wife-to-be:

- M.A., Experimental Psychology, California State University, Fullerton

- Ph.D., Psychology, UCLA with emphases in personality psychology, social psychology, and measurement and psychometrics

- Chair, Department of Psychology and Behavioral Science at Canadian University College in Lacombe, Alberta

- Professor of Psychology specializing in personality psychology, social psychology, pre-marital counseling, and research methods

- Author of *SPSS for Windows, Step by Step*, academic best seller in its 9th edition, published in three languages and distributed in eighty countries.

- Author of numerous articles dealing with relational success and helping behavior

- U.S. Olympic Trials finalist in the marathon, MVP of the 30 Km. National Championship Team

But how could they know they'd be happy together? After all, the single greatest factor in life happiness is the quality of the marriage relationship, and neither had experienced success in that regard. The answer to that question is *The Compatibility Code*. Together they combined success principles with research psychology to create this easy–to-follow partner selection code that helps women reduce the risk in dating, increases their confidence in finding the right person, and equips them with tools to improve their choice. Darren and Elizabeth have now facilitated hundreds of interactive groups addressing pre-marital success, marital compatibility, communication, and conflict resolution. They don't help you fall in love; they help you stride confidently forward and connect with the person you know is right for you.

For more information visit www.TheCompatibilityCode.com.

SPECIAL BONUS
for Readers of *The Compatibility Code*

Congratulations!!! You've decided to lead with your head before you follow your heart. This captures the essence of the *Compatibility Code's* value for you. It is a book that should be used as well as read!

Darren and I recognize that some of you might hesitate to write in and on your copy of *The Compatibility Code*. And many of you will simply need more room to write and record your journey. After all, you might go through this process of discovery with more than one "candidate!"

With that in mind, we'd like to offer you a Special Bonus download of *The Compatibility Code Handbook*. Your Special Bonus contains:

1. The *Compatibility Code* Short Course, a quick-fire version of the book, and

2. All the forms and worksheets contained in the book.

You can download the *Handbook* as many times as you like. Whether you need spare worksheets for yourself—or you need extras for a friend— you will never run out of room for your responses. By the way, this might be a good time to consider leading several of your friends in a *Compatibility Code* girls' group. What a great way to share this incredible experience with women you care about!

TO DOWNLOAD YOUR SPECIAL BONUS TODAY:

- Visit us online at www.TheCompatibilityCode.com/bonus
- Enter the bonus code TCCSB
- Enter your name and e-mail address

That's it! A link for the download will be sent immediately to your Inbox. Do it today!

Best wishes for a love that will last a lifetime!

Elizabeth and Darren George

BUY A SHARE OF THE FUTURE IN YOUR COMMUNITY

These certificates make great holiday, graduation and birthday gifts that can be personalized with the recipient's name. The cost of one S.H.A.R.E. or one square foot is $54.17. The personalized certificate is suitable for framing and will state the number of shares purchased and the amount of each share, as well as the recipient's name. The home that you participate in "building" will last for many years and will continue to grow in value.

Here is a sample SHARE certificate:

YES, I WOULD LIKE TO HELP!

*I support the work that Habitat for Humanity does and I want to be part of the excitement! As a donor, I will receive periodic updates on your construction activities but, more importantly, I know my gift will help a family in our community realize the dream of homeownership. **I would like to SHARE in your efforts against substandard housing in my community!** (Please print below)*

PLEASE SEND ME _____ SHARES at $54.17 EACH = $ $_____

In Honor Of: _____

Occasion: (Circle One)   HOLIDAY   BIRTHDAY   ANNIVERSARY

    OTHER: _____

Address of Recipient: _____

Gift From: _____ *Donor Address:* _____

Donor Email: _____

I AM ENCLOSING A CHECK FOR $ $_____ PAYABLE TO HABITAT FOR HUMANITY <u>OR</u> PLEASE CHARGE MY VISA OR MASTERCARD *(CIRCLE ONE)*

Card Number _____ Expiration Date: _____

Name as it appears on Credit Card _____ Charge Amount $ _____

Signature _____

Billing Address _____

Telephone # Day _____ Eve _____

PLEASE NOTE: Your contribution is tax-deductible to the fullest extent allowed by law.
Habitat for Humanity • P.O. Box 1443 • Newport News, VA 23601 • 757-596-5553
www.HelpHabitatforHumanity.org